Philosophy and the Idea of Freedom

Philosophy and the Eclipse of Reason:
Towards a Metacritique of the Philosophical Tradition

Philosophy and the Idea of Freedom

ROY BHASKAR

BLACKWELL
Oxford UK & Cambridge USA

First published 1991

Basil Blackwell Ltd
108 Cowley Road, Oxford, OX4 1JF, UK

Basil Blackwell, Inc.
3 Cambridge Center
Cambridge, Massachusetts 02142, USA

Library of Congress Cataloging in Publication Data

Bhaskar, Roy, 1944–
  Philosophy and the idea of freedom / Roy Bhaskar.
      p.   cm. — (Philosophy and the eclipse of reason; v. 1)
  Includes bibliographical references and index.
  ISBN 0–631–15911–8 — ISBN 0–631–17082–0 (pbk.)
    1. Rorty, Richard.   2. Realism.   3.Social sciences—Philosophy.
  4. Ethics.   5. Philosophy, Marxist.   I. Title.   II. Series:
  Bhaskar, Roy, 1944– Philosophy and the eclipse of reason; v. 1.
  B21.B48   1991 vol. 1
  [B945.R524]
  149'.2 s–dc20
  [191]
                                                                    90–27536
                                                                        CIP

British Library Cataloguing in Publication Data

A CIP catalogue record for this book is available from the British Library.

Typeset in 11 on 13 pt Palatino
by Graphicraft Typesetters, Hong Kong
Printed in Great Britain by T. J. Press Ltd, Padstow, Cornwall.

This book is printed on acid-free paper.

Contents

Contents

Preface

A liberal society is one which has no ideal except freedom.
Richard Rorty, 'The contingency of community'

Section One of this book is essentially a critique of the work of Richard Rorty, who has given us an eloquent critique of the epistemological problematic, from which contemporary philosophy is gradually emerging. But I want to suggest that he has provided us with only a partial critique of a problem-field, to which he remains in crucial respects captive. These passing notes are not of course innocent. They are written from a particular perspective, that of a Lockean underlabouring interest in human sciences, which partly do and partly do not (yet) exist – which are in the process of struggling to come into being. Such sciences would provide that sort of consciousness of our natural and social past and present as to allow us to change both ourselves and the conditions under which we live (cf. PMN, p. 359) in such a way that 'the distinction between the reformer and the (violent) revolutionary is no longer necessary' (CC, p. 13). More specifically, I want to claim that we shall only be able 'to see how things, in the broadest possible sense of the term, hang together, in the broadest possible sense of the term' (CP, p. xiv) from this perspective if we are committed to:

1 an *ontologically*-oriented, philosophically realist account of science, on which the world is explicitly construed, contrary to Humean ontology, as structured, differentiated and changing; and

2 a *critical* naturalist account of the human sciences, which will sustain the idea of an explanatory critique of specific structural sources of determination and their emancipatory transformation.

Rorty remains, I am going to contend, a prisoner of the implicit ontology of the problematic he describes. My aim is to carry the dialectic of 'de-divinization' (cf. CC, p. 10) a stage or two further, by conceiving reality, being, the world (precisely as it is known to us in science) as only *contingently* related to human beings; and therefore as not *essentially* characterizable as either empirical or rational or in terms of any other human attribute. This is the mistake of what I call the 'epistemic fallacy': the definition of being in terms of knowledge (RTS, pp. 36ff). A picture has indeed held philosophy captive.* It is a picture of ourselves or our insignia in any picture – the picture as invariably containing our mirror-image or mark. Philosophical post-narcissism (cf. CS, p. 12) will be evinced in the exercise of our capacity to draw non-anthropomorphic pictures of being. This is my main post-Rortian point.

But I shall also be pursuing one or two subsidiary theses. I shall argue that Rorty's remarks on science reveal an unacceptable positivist–instrumentalist and Humean–Hempelian bias, and that his account of science is based on a half-truth. Further, I shall contend that *Philosophy and the Mirror of Nature* is characterized by a central tension – roughly that of Kant's '"existentialist" distinction between people as empirical selves and as moral agents' (PMN, p. 382), a fault line parallel to that of the Kantian resolution of the third antinomy, on which PMN is 'stuck fast'. Moreover, as in Kant's case, it is Rorty's ontology that is responsible for his failure to sustain an adequate account of agency and *a fortiori* of freedom as involving *inter alia* emancipation from real and scientifically knowable specific constraints, rather than merely the poetic

* L. Wittgenstein, *Philosophical Investigations*, I § 115, Oxford, 1963.

redescription of an already determined world. I shall also be contending that *Contingency, irony and solidarity*, Rorty's latest book, is likewise 'stuck fast' on an antinomy – within this antinomy – roughly, that between private perfection and public happiness – in effect between Kant's 'two duties for men'.

Section Two contains three texts to complement this critique of Rorty. The first situates critical realism, the philosophical standpoint from which I approach Rorty, in the context of our philosophical times. The second clarifies the relations between fact and value, theory and practice, explanation and emancipation. The third is a synoptic digest of the tradition of Marxist philosophy – a topic on which Rorty is extremely ill-informed – from Karl Marx to Louis Althusser.

This book itself is the first volume of a three-volume study on the trajectory of the western philosophical tradition and the state of contemporary philosophy. In this study I shall argue that certain pervasive assumptions about the nature of knowledge, the world and their relations underpin the philosophical tradition and inform much contemporary culture, including the practice of social science. In their standard forms, these assumptions are that knowledge is or must be incorrigible and permanent, that the world is essentially unstructured, undifferentiated and unchanging, and that the relationship between knowledge and the world is one of isomorphism or even identity, i.e. such that knowledge replicates, mirrors and reflects the world. These assumptions are undergirded by the epistemic fallacy. And underlying these mistakes are certain prevalent misconceptions about the nature of human beings and society.

In the volumes to come I shall show just why this ensemble of assumptions is false, and analyse some of its contemporary manifestations. I shall also be showing how the critical realist account of reality can be applied to the social world and its investigation itself. The upshot of the trilogy is a view of social science as essentially critical (and self-critical), and as having, through its explanatory power, emancipatory implications for substantive social life itself.

Roy Bhaskar   22 November 1990*

* The date of Mrs Thatcher's resignation as Prime Minister.

Acknowledgements

My thanks are due to Basil Blackwell and Alan Malachowski for permission to reprint material that initially appeared in *Reading Rorty* (Oxford, 1990). Thanks are also due to Philip Carpenter for his immense patience and unfailing support in this project; to Ruth Kimber for copy-editing and to Andrew McNeillie for steering the book through the editorial process; and to the team at Basil Blackwell for the prompt and efficient publication of this book. I have received much stimulation and encouragement over the past few years from the annual conferences on Realism in the Human Sciences. I am particularly indebted to Sue Kelly for invaluable secretarial assistance; and to William Outhwaite, Andrew Collier and Hilary Wainwright for the rigour of their intellectual sustenance and the warmth of their personal friendship. ·

A word on the provenance of the materials in Section Two may be helpful. Chapter 9 is based on a talk originally given at a symposium organized by the Institute of Contemporary Arts on 'What is Critical Realism?' in London in December 1989. Appendix 1 was first presented to the 12th World Congress of Sociology in Madrid in July 1990. Appendix 2 was commissioned as an Afterword to a collection of essays by Louis Althusser and composed in January 1989.

Abbreviations in the text

Works by Richard Rorty

CC   'The contingency of community', *London Review of Books*, 24 July 1986.
CIS *Contingency, irony and solidarity*, Cambridge, 1989.
CL   'The contingency of language', *London Review of Books*, 17 April 1986.
CP   *The Consequences of Pragmatism*, Brighton, 1982.
CS   'The contingency of self', *London Review of Books*, 8 May 1986.
DC   'Deconstruction and circumvention', in *Critical Inquiry*, September 1984.
FMR 'Freud and moral reflection', in *Pragmatism's Freud: the moral disposition of psychoanalysis*, ed. J. H. Smith and W. Kerrigan, Baltimore, 1986.
HLP 'Habermas and Lyotard on postmodernity', in *Habermas and Modernity*, ed. R. Bernstein, Cambridge, 1985.
LT   *The Linguistic Turn*, ed. R. Rorty, Chicago, 1967.
NL   Northcliffe Lectures, 1986.
PBL 'Postmodernist bourgeois liberalism', *The Journal of Philosophy* 80, October 1983.
PDP 'The priority of democracy to philosophy', in *Reading Rorty*, ed. A. Malachowski, Oxford, 1990.
PMN *Philosophy and the Mirror of Nature*, Oxford, 1980.

SO   'Solidarity or objectivity?', in *Post-Analytic Philosophy*, ed. J. Rajchman and C. West, New York, 1985.
TM   'Realism and reference', *The Monist*, Vol. 59, 1976.
TT   'Thugs and theorists', in *Political Theory*, Vol. 15, November 1987.

Work by Richard Bernstein

OSF   'One step forward, two steps backwards', in *Political Theory*, Vol. 15, November 1987.

Work edited by Alan Malachowski

AM   *Reading Rorty*, ed. Alan Malachowski, Oxford, 1990.

Works by Roy Bhaskar

PON   *The Possibility of Naturalism*, 1st edn, Brighton, 1979; 2nd edn, Hemel Hempstead, 1989.
RR   *Reclaiming Reality*, London, 1989.
RTS   *A Realist Theory of Science*, 1st edn, Leeds 1975; 2nd edn, Brighton, 1978 [Hemel Hempstead 1989].
SR   *Scientific Realism and Human Emancipation*, London, 1986.

Section One

Anti-Rorty

Part I

Knowledge

1

Rorty's Account of Science

The first step is the one that altogether escapes notice. We talk of processes and states and leave their nature undecided. Sometime perhaps we shall know more about them – we think. But this is just what commits us to a particular way of looking at the matter. For we have a definite concept of what it means to know a process better. (The decisive move in the conjuring trick has been made, and it was the very one we thought quite innocent.)
L. Wittgenstein, *Philosophical Investigations* I, § 308

'Kuhn himself . . . occasionally makes too large concessions to the tradition, particularly when he suggests there is a serious and unresolved problem about why the scientific enterprise has been doing so nicely lately' (PMN, p. 339). Rorty goes on to diagnose the unease felt by Kuhn at the absence of a solution to the problem of induction as merely the expression of 'a certain inarticulate dissatisfaction' (PMN, p. 341). Still, this does raise the issue of the characterization of science. I shall suggest shortly that Rorty seriously underdescribes science; that he gives too 'thin' and impoverished a description of it, perhaps because he is bored by it. But in the meantime we can at least press the question as to *in what* science is presumed to have been so successful of late. It transpires that this lies in the 'prediction and control of nature' (PMN, p. 341;

cf. PMN, p. 356; CP, p. 140; CIS, p. 4). Rorty assumes that the
aim of science is prediction, manipulation and control – Com-
tean 'savoir pour prévoir, prévoir pour pouvoir'; and that
explanation is deductive-subsumptive and symmetrical with
prediction, i.e. Hempelian in form (PMN, pp. 347, 356; CP,
chapter 11). This is a bias he shares with Habermas.[1] Such
explanations presuppose, of course, Humean causal laws. The
truth of physicalism and regularity (Humean) determinism
(PMN, pp. 38n, 205, 354, 387) is rendered consistent with the
truth of non-physicalistic statements by reference to Davidsonian theory, on which singular causal claims or heteronomic
(non-strictly Humean) generalizations entail that a homonomic, strictly Humean description exists.[2] Thus Rorty is committed to a quintessentially *positivist* account of the logical
form of sentences in science, and of the structure of scientific
theories. This in turn presupposes that the world is at least
fundamentally (though not necessarily exclusively) Humean–
Laplacean in form, i.e. constituted by atomistic events or
states of affairs or molecular state descriptions and their *constant conjunctions.*

That Rorty can presuppose as much has to be explained by
a critical lacuna in his dialectical reconstruction of the recent
history of analytical philosophy of science. Roughly speaking,
there have been two main axes of criticism of the canonical
positivist view of science against which Wittgensteinians,
Popperians and Kuhnians reacted. There has been criticism of
its *monistic* theory of scientific development, turning on the
social, historical and/or discontinuous character of scientific
knowledge – of the kind advanced by Sellars, Feyerabend and
Kuhn. But there has also been criticism, from Scriven on, of
the *deductivist* theory of scientific structure, turning especially
on the stratification of scientific knowledge. Although Rorty is
aware of this strand of criticism (see PMN, p. 168),[3] it plays no
real role in his narrative.[4] It is a strand that is especially salient
for debates about the *Geisteswissenschaften*, where explanations
conforming to the deductive-nomological model are totally
unforthcoming[5] and where any generalizations have to be
formulated 'normically', i.e. so as to allow for exceptions.[6]

There are two main moments in the anti-deductivist critique of Humean and Hempelian theory. The first, whose prototype was provided by Kant's critique of Hume, which was later repeated in refracted forms by Campbell's critique of Duhem, and then by Hesse's and Harré's critiques of Hempel,[7] involves the denial that constant conjunctions are *sufficient* for causal laws, explanations, scientific theories. But it is the second on which I wish to fasten here. It involves the denial that constant conjunctions are even *necessary*. This 'transcendental realist' stance may be motivated by reflection on the nature of experimental and applied scientific activity (see RTS, chapters 1 and 2). Analysis of experimental activity shows that the regularities required for the empirical identification of laws hold only under special and in general artificially produced closed conditions; but, for at least a large class of fundamental laws,[8] analysis of applied activity shows that these laws are presumed to prevail in open systems, i.e. outside the conditions that permit their empirical identification, where no constant conjunctions obtain. Such laws have to be analysed *transfactually*, i.e. as tendencies. These tendencies are of novel kinds of entity, imposing constraints on the familiar world of human being-sized material things. They are the relatively enduring generative mechanisms and structures of nature, initially hypothesized in the scientific imagination, but sometimes subsequently discovered to be real, which produce the flux of events. There are no known laws in physics which conform to the Humean schema. Generalizations can be empirical, or more broadly actual, or universal, but not both – a consequence that Cartwright captures in the title of her book, *How the Laws of Physics Lie*.[9]

Transcendental (or, as I have also called it, critical) realism (see RR, chapter 9) makes possible a reformulation of the dusty old Greek action/contemplation contrast (PMN, p. 11). There is 'a difference which makes a difference' between (a) 'it works because it's true' and (b) 'it's true because it works' (CP, p. xxxix). (a) gives the gist of applied explanations in open systems; (b) of theoretical corroborations in closed systems. (Nor is it the case that 'every difference must *make* a difference' (CP, p. xxxv) – for the same effect may be produced by a plurality of different (and even changing) structures or mechanisms; just as the same structure (or mechanism) may generate (under different circumstances) a variety of different effects (cf. PON 2, p. 176).) Rorty notes that Newtonian mechanics was doubly paradigmatic for the founders of modern philosophy – as 'a method for finding truth' and 'a model for the mechanics of inner space' (PMN, p. 328n). But he remains under the spell of a third effect of the celestial closure achieved by Newtonian mechanics: namely, its forming a model of phenomena as well as a template for science, an ontological paradigm of an empirical actualist and regularity determinist cast. Galileo and Newton were misinterpreted by the Enlightenment. It is important to appreciate that in the battle between the gods and the giants (CP, p. xv), the friends of the Earth (the positivists) no less than the friends of the Forms (the Platonists) have been wrong about science.

Reflection on experimental and applied scientific activity reveals that science is committed to a non-anthropocentric and specifically non-Humean ontology – of structures and generative mechanisms irreducible to and often out of phase with the (normally artificially contrived) patterns of events which comprise their empirical grounds. In particular, the laws of nature, as they are currently known to us, entail the (contingently counterfactual) possibility of a non-human world, and thus a world without science; that is, that they would operate even if they were unknown, just as they continue to operate (transfactually) outside the closed conditions which enable their empirical identification in science. It follows from this that statements about being cannot be reduced to or analysed or explicated in terms of statements about knowledge, so that what I have referred to as the 'epistemic fallacy' – the definition of being in terms of knowledge (see RTS, pp. 36ff) – *is* a fallacy (cf. SR, p. 47). Accordingly, we need two dimensions in which to talk about science: an ontological or 'intransitive' dimension and an epistemological or historical sociological or 'transitive' dimension (cf. RTS, chapter 1.1). The laws of nature, unlike their normally experimentally produced grounds, are not empirical, but they are none the less real (tendencies). That the reality known to us in science is only contingently related to our experience, and knowledge of it and, more generally, human being is the only position consistent with a 'scientific realist' (PMN, p. 381) world-view or congruent with the Sellarsian dictum, which Rorty quotes approvingly, that 'science is the measure of all things, of what is that it is, and of what is not that it is not.'[10]

One consequence of the argument which establishes the transfactual and non-empirical nature of laws is that a philosophical as distinct from a sociological ontology is *irreducible* in the philosophy of science. A philosophical ontology will consist of some general account of the world, e.g. to the effect that it is structured, differentiated and changing, whereas a scientific ontology will specify the structures which, according to the science of the day, it contains and the particular ways they are differentiated and changing (see RTS, p. 29).[11] But a moment's reflection will show that a philosophical ontology is *inevitable* too, for one cannot talk about science – for instance, about the logical form of causal laws – without implicitly or explicitly presupposing something about the world known by science – that is, about its ontological form, say to the effect that it is constituted by events which are constantly conjoined in space and over time. Commitment to empirical realism, and in particular to the Humean theory of causal laws (empirical invariances as necessary or necessary and sufficient for causal laws), carries with it commitment to a (false) general account of the world.

A very damaging feature of empirical realism is its systematic tendency to conflate knowledge and being, as in the notion of the 'empirical world', or to run together epistemological and ontological concepts and concerns. Thus the transfactuality of laws is just one aspect of the existential intransitivity of objects – the condition that in general things exist (and act) independently of our experience, description and knowledge of them (and, for the most part, of our means of epistemic access to them). (This is consistent with regional causal interdependency in the processes of the production of things and their descriptions, e.g. in the social domain (cf. PON 1, p. 60; PON 2, p. 47).) The idea of the existential intransitivity of objects (as a proposition in the intransitive dimension of the philosophy of science) is (strongly) compatible with the idea of the social production of knowledge (as a proposition in the transitive dimension of the philosophy of science). Paradigmatically, we *make* facts and, in experimental activity, closed systems; but *find* out about (i.e. discover, identify and investigate the nature and properties of) things, structures and causal laws (cf. CL, p. 3; CIS, p. 3; CP, p. xxxix; PMN, p. 344). We could stipulate these are 'necessary truths', but it is probably better to recognize that there is an inherent ambiguity or bipolarity in our use of terms like 'causes', 'laws', 'facts' (and even 'truths' (cf. SR, p. 99)) and to be prepared, whenever necessary, to disambiguate them, distinguishing the transitive (social or making) from the intransitive (ontological or finding) employment of these terms.

Kuhn furnishes a famous case of transitive–intransitive (epistemological–ontological) ambiguity when he notoriously says, in a passage discussed by Rorty (PMN, pp. 344–5), that we must learn to make sense of sentences like this: 'Though the world does not change with a change of paradigm, the scientist afterward works in a different world.'[12] Once we disambiguate 'the world' into 'social, historical, transitive' and 'natural, (relatively) unchanging, intransitive' we can transcribe the sentence, without paradox, as: 'Though the (natural (or object)) world does not change with a change of paradigm, the scientist afterward works in a different (social or (cognitive)) world.' (Cf. RR, pp. 196–7 n. 79.) I shall suggest in a moment that Rorty's argument trades in places on a similar (or even the identical) ambiguity and paradox.

A consequence of the non-anthropocentric ontology to which science, but not Rorty, is committed is that it is not optional, but mandatory that we tell causal stories which make the laws of physics prior to and longer than the truths of biology and both of these the backdrop for human history. It is not just 'hard' but inconsistent with the historical emergence, practical presuppositions and substantive content of the sciences 'to tell a story of changing physical universes against the background of an unchanging Moral Law or poetic canon' (PMN, pp. 344–5).

In any event, 'physics gives us a good background against which to tell our stories of historical change' (PMN, p. 345) is ambiguous in the way of Kuhn's 'world'. If physics means 'the physical world' as described by the science of physics (i.e. physics$_{id}$ – or the physical world), then it is unparadoxical and true. If, however, physics means 'the set of descriptions' of the physical world in the science of physics (i.e. physics$_{td}$ – or the science of physics), then as a rapidly changing social product, it is part of the process of historical change and so cannot form a background to it.

Some further instances of this ambiguity may be usefully documented. At PMN, p. 342, Rorty claims that the reduction of the cognitive (fact, theory) to the non-cognitive (value, practice) would seem to '"spiritualize" nature by making it like history or literature, something which men have *made* rather than *found*', whereas it would merely spiritualize (natural) science, which has indeed been made rather than found. (The identity of nature and science only obtains if one perpetrates the epistemic fallacy, or subscribes to the subject–object identity theory with which that fallacy is implicated – in which indeed it is founded.) In CS, p. 11 (and CIS, p. 28), finessing the Nietzschean view of self-knowledge as self-creation, Rorty remarks that 'the only way to trace home the causes of one being as one is would be tell a story about one's causes in a new language.' He continues: 'This may sound paradoxical, because we think of causes being discovered rather than invented. . . . But even in the natural sciences we occasionally get genuinely new causal stories, the sort of story produced by what Kuhn calls "revolutionary science".' However what are told in revolutionary science are new – revolutionary – stories$_{td}$ about the causes$_{id}$ of natural phenomena. Moreover, in social life the principle of existential intransitivity holds just the same. Thus redescribing$_{td}$ the past in a revolutionary way can cause$_{id}$ radical new changes, including a new sense of identity, self-definition or auto-biography. But it cannot retrospectively cause$_{id}$ old changes, i.e. alter the past as distinct from its interpretation. It is not surprising that Rorty should slip from transitive to intransitive uses of terms like 'cause' – it is endemic to empirical realism, the epistemological definition of being in terms of (a particular empiricist concept of) experience.

Again, discussing at CP, p. 199 a hermeneutical position to the effect that interpretation in the human sciences 'begins from the postulate that the web of meaning constitutes human existence', Rorty claims that 'this suggests that a fossil (for example) might get constituted *without* a web of meanings'. But this glosses over the difference between epistemic constitution$_{td}$ and ontic constitution$_{id}$, the sense in which all sciences alike are meaningful or conceptually/linguistically constituted$_{td}$ and the sense in which the *subject-matter* of the human, but *not* the non-human, sciences, is already at least partially meaningful or conceptually/linguistically constituted$_{id}$, necessitating a 'double hermeneutic' in them (cf. PON 1, p. 199; PON 2, pp. 134–5).[13] Rorty's neglect of ontology (as well, as we shall see, as his concept of a person) leads him to overlook the way in which social life is pre-interpreted and conceptualized prior to and irrespective of any enquiry, so that he hypernaturalistically fails to 'see any interesting difference between what [Galileo and Darwin] were doing and what biblical exigetics, literary critics or historians of culture do' (CP, p. 199).

Rorty's seminal 1972 paper 'The world well lost' (CP, chapter 1) yields a final example of transitive–intransitive ambiguity. In it, Rorty maintains that ' "the world" is either the purely vacuous notion of the ineffable cause of sense and goal of intellect, or else a name for the objects that enquiry for the moment is leaving alone, those planks in the boat that are not being moved about', adding that 'epistemology since Kant has shuttled back and forth between these two meanings of the term "world" ' (CP, p. 15). Rorty wants to jettison the former 'transcendent' use of the term. But in plumping for the latter, 'immanent' use, Rorty fails to notice the systematic equivocation *within* it, viz. between the intransitive objects$_{id}$ of our investigation, known by but in general independent of us (the 'objects of enquiry') and the transitive cognitive results$_{td}$ of those investigations, the planks in Neurath's boat (which may, of course, become the objects of various meta-epistemic enquiries (cf. SR, p. 37)). Why do we need the notion of intransitive objects$_{id}$ of enquiry, as distinct from transitive results$_{td}$? To make sense of (a) our cognitive practices (the ways we change and augment the planks in the boat); (b) the uses of knowledge (the cognition-dependent activities – fishing, ferrying, cruising – in which we seafarers engage; and (c) the historical formation of the sciences (the processes by which the boat got built in the first place and might yet get sunk).

I have been arguing that Rorty remains committed to empirical realism, and the epistemic fallacy it enshrines, and that he *de facto* inherits a positivist ontology in virtue of his subscription to a Humean–Hempelian account of science (albeit as modified by Davidson); that is to say, he tacitly *misdescribes* science. But it is equally important to see that Rorty damagingly *underdescribes* science, generally reducing it to a mere instance of discourse, of the 'linguistified'. This not only abstracts from the material aspects of science (such as experimental activity) but from the specificity of scientific as distinct from other kinds of discourse, and the internal differentiations (e.g. pure/applied, natural/human) within science itself. This results in a hypernaturalistic linguistified monism or pantextualism,[14] relieved at best by distinctions between normal and abnormal discourse and/or scientific and literary cultures.[15] In addition, and directly flowing from his minimalist misdescription of science, Rorty (a) a-rationalizes the history of science, (b) ignores the continuity between philosophy and science, and (c) overlooks the possible impact of his philosophical 'kibitzing' (CP, p. 221; PMN, p. 393) on science, especially on the fraught human sciences, where Rorty's 'joshing' (PDP, p. 293) may be taken very seriously indeed.

Rorty tends to operate with a notion of discursive activity organized around a single fault-line: that between poetic and normal or literal discourse, where a poet is 'one who makes

things new' (CIS, p. 12).[16] Rorty forgets that the whole point
of the concept of a 'language-game' is that language-games (or
more generally, practices) *differ*. There can be no presumption
that what is philosophically significant about these differences
can be reduced to the single axis or dimension of variation
given by the distinction between 'normal' and 'abnormal' discourse (see PMN, p. 333; CP, p. 106) (itself abstracted from
the Kuhnian distinction between 'normal' and 'abnormal' science) or by the distinctions between the old and the new, or
the literal and the unfamiliar.

Thus in CL and CIS Rorty claims that

> we often let the world decide the competition between alterna-
> tive sentences (e.g. between 'Red wins' and 'Black wins' or
> between 'The butler did it' and 'The doctor did it') . . . But it is
> not so easy when we turn from individual sentences to vocabu-
> laries as wholes. When we consider examples of alternative
> language-games – the vocabulary of ancient Athenian politics
> versus Jefferson's, the moral vocabulary of Saint Paul versus
> Freud's, the jargon of Newton versus that of Aristotle, the
> idiom of Blake versus that of Dryden – it is difficult to think of
> the world making one of these better than another, of the
> world deciding between the two. (CIS, p. 5; cf. CL, p. 3)

Now as Tom Sorell has remarked: 'It is misleading to say that
[the clash between Aristotle and Newton] was merely a clash
of vocabularies [or jargons] . . . It was a clash of theories, of
assertions of certain explanations of phenomena, phrased in
different vocabularies. Between different theories the world
sometimes *can* decide, for example, by making the predictions
of one true and the other false' (AM, p. 19). Sorell continues:

> The impression that perhaps the world cannot decide between
> Newton and Aristotle is encouraged by treating the differences
> between them as a specimen of a difference equally well illus-
> trated by Jefferson and the Athenians, Freud and St Paul, and
> Blake and Dryden. But that there is not just one kind of dif-
> ference is shown by the fact that Newton's and Aristotle's
> 'jargons' can be contrasted in terms of predictive accuracy,

whereas the others cannot. No doubt it is true that a clash of vocabularies runs throughout Rorty's examples. Difference of vocabulary is the lowest common denominator; the point is that it may be *too* low when what is at issue is whether the world can decide between what is said in different vocabularies. No-one expects the world to choose between different lexicons but the world can and does decide between theories.

And, one might go on, it is precisely because of this that one can rationally justify the choice of one – Newton's – rather than another – Aristotle's – vocabulary here.

Charles Taylor makes a related point in arguing against the Rortian claim that the differences between language-games are unarbitrable:

> There are some issues in the long history of western thought which have been settled. For instance, a science which tried to explain inanimate nature in terms of the realization in different kinds of entity of their corresponding Form has given way to a science which explains by efficient causation, mapped by mathematical formulae. Aristotle on this issue has been buried by Galileo and Newton, and there is no turning back. . . . This shows that Rorty's belief that the world doesn't 'decide between' language-games isn't . . . an empirically established thesis. On the contrary, issues that have been quite conclusively decided rationally . . . are re-interpreted [by Rorty] as having been settled on pragmatic grounds. (AM, p. 262)

Or, one might add, even by accident (cf. CIS, p. 17) or luck (cf. CP, p. 193).

Rorty's claim, tacitly appealing to Kuhn (and also to Davidson – for whom rationality can be glossed as 'internal coherence'), is that there are no rational criteria which would enable an impartial observer to decide between incommensurable paradigms – for rationality is paradigm-, language-game- or vocabulary-specific. Now it is doubtful whether or not this is a correct interpretation of Kuhn.[17] For there are, buried in his work, criteria (including accuracy of predictions, number of problems solved, etc.) strong enough to sustain a rational judgement of, say, Einstein over Newton and Galileo over Aristotle, although Kuhn draws back from acknowledging this – a phenomenon we may refer to as 'Kuhn-blindness' (see RR, chapter 3, especially pp. 196–7, n. 79). Moreover, even in the limiting case where the vocabularies of the antagonists are totally incommensurable, there are criteria capable of sustaining judgements of, say, trustworthiness rather than mere novelty – namely, one will prefer that theory which is capable of explaining more or more significant phenomena in its own terms than the others do in theirs (see RTS, p. 248; RR, pp. 32–3; SR, chapter 1.6). Finally, epistemic relativism and historicism are quite consistent with judgemental rationalism and logical rigour (PON 1, p. 73; PON 2, pp. 57–8; RR, pp. 23–4).

In fact, by the time of NL (1986), and even more so CIS (1989), Rorty's position has become both Kuhn-blind and confused. Thus at CIS, p. 99, Rorty declares that 'although [a] the thorough-going ironist can use the notion of a "better description", [b] he has no criteria for the application of this term and so [c] cannot use the notion of "the right description".' In line with [b], Rorty says that there cannot be 'reasons for using languages as well as reasons within languages for believing statements' (CIS, p. 48) or 'agreement on good reasons for using new languages, as opposed to good reasons, within old languages, for believing statements within those languages' (CC, p. 10). But earlier, at CIS, p. 20 (and CL, p. 6), we are given precisely such a reason when it is allowed that 'a Galilean vocabulary enables us to make better predictions than an Aristotelean vocabulary' (it being denied merely that we can infer from this that 'the book of nature is written in the language of mathematics' (ibid.)). Moreover, it is difficult to see how the efficiency of tools (vocabularies) can be evaluated or compared (CIS, p. 11), or interference between different tools registered (CIS, p. 12) except in relation to some sort of yardstick, measure or objective function – in which case we have – *contra* [b] – criteria for the application of the term 'better description'.

Rorty not only misdescribes and underdescribes science, he dislikes the philosophical culture that has grown up with and around it since the seventeenth century. In CIS, p. 52, he says:

> It was natural for liberal political thought in the eighteenth century to try to associate itself with the most promising cultural development of the time, the natural sciences. But unfortunately the Enlightenment wove much of its political rhetoric around a picture of the scientist as a sort of priest, someone who achieved contact with the non-human truth by being 'logical', 'methodical' and 'objective'.... This was a useful tactic in its day, but it is less useful nowadays. For, in the first place, the sciences are no longer the most interesting or promising or exciting area of culture. In the second place, historians of science have made clear how little this picture of the scientist has to do with actual scientific achievement, how pointless it is to try to isolate something called 'the scientific method'. Although the sciences have burgeoned a thousandfold since the end of the eighteenth century, and have thereby made possible the realization of political goals which could never have been realized without them, they have nevertheless receded into the background of cultural life. This recession is due largely to the increasing difficulty of mastering the various languages in which all the various sciences are conducted. It is not something to be deplored but, rather, something to be coped with. We can do so by switching attention to the areas which *are* at the forefront of culture, those which excite the imagination of the young, namely, art and utopian politics.

In CP a contrast between scientific and literary cultures dominates the stage. (This opposition is displaced in PMN onto the contrast between epistemology and hermeneutics, and in CIS onto that between metaphysics and irony. In each case the second term is usually seen as reactive to or parasitic upon the first (see CP, p. 137; PMN, pp. 366–9; and CIS, pp. 87–8 – but see also PMN, p. 394 for the suggestion of the possibility of a purely edifying philosophy and CIS, p. xv, for that of universal ironism).) This distinction is associated with three others:

1 between normal and abnormal discourse;
2 between banausic (CP, p. 142), quasi-algorithmic or para-mechanical and creative redescriptive practices; and
3 between philosophy as a Fach (CP, p. 22; cf. PMN, p. 381) and post-Philosophical culture criticism (CP, p. xl; cf. CIS, p. 82).

The whole tendency in CP is to reduce and replace the contrast science/non-science to and with the contrast between normal and abnormal discourse (CP, p. 106; cf. PMN, p. 333), itself likened to the contrast between normal and deviant sexual practices (CP, p. 106) – scientific culture being tacitly assimilated to the former normal pole and literature, which succeeds 'without argument', 'simply by its success' (CP, p. 142) to the latter. From this standpoint all that can be said about great scientific transitions is that they comprise success-ful (taken up and habitualized) abnormal discourse. Revolu-tionary scientists like Galileo 'just lucked out' (CP, p. 193). Thus 'from a fully-fledged pragmatist point of view, there is no interesting difference between tables and texts, between protons and poems' (CP, p. 153). Indeed, from the perspec-tive of the literary intellectual, 'quantum mechanics [is] a notoriously great, but quite untranslatable, poem written in a lamentably obscure language' (CP, p. 67).

In denigrating the philosophical culture around science, Rorty is anxious not to denigrate science. For its 'discoveries are the basis of modern technological civilization. We can hardly be too grateful for them' (CP, p. 191). Rather, we should try to approach a position where we can see 'modern physics both as [C. P.] Snow sees it – as the greatest human accomplishment of the century – and as Kuhn sees it, as one more episode in a series of crises and intervening calms, a series that will never terminate in "the discovery of truth, the finally accurate representation of reality"' (CP, p. 87). Science is not to be erected into 'an idol to fill the place once held by God. [Rather science is] one genre of literature – or, put the other way round, literature and the arts [are] enquiries, on the same footing as scientific enquiries' (CP, p. xliii).[18] 'Physics is a matter of trying to cope with various bits of the universe; ethics is a matter of trying to cope with other bits' (CP, p. xliii).

It seems clear that Rorty wants a post-Philosophical but not a post-scientific culture. But what if this philosophical culture, or a reformed part of it, is a necessary condition for the sciences themselves? What if, in Bernard Williams' words, 'the descriptions he dislikes come from within science itself' (AM, p. 30)? Rorty thinks that modern science can survive without its ideology, forged in the Enlightenment (PMN, pp. 333n, 328n), whereas modern literature, paradoxically, may not.[19] But can Rorty's message be neutral (or perhaps even edifying, or otherwise advantageous) for modern science? It seems highly unlikely that the 'language-game' 'of the informed dilettante, the polypragmatic, Socratic intermediary between various discourses', in whose 'salon ... hermetic thinkers are charmed out of their self-enclosed practices' (PMN, p. 317) – Rorty's job description for the new post-Philosophical and non-epistemological philosopher – can leave, in Wittgenstein's phrase, 'everything as it was'.[20] The assumption that it could, would seem to ignore the continuity and two-way traffic between philosophy and science; to over-look the extent to which the 'diurnal' philosophy of the scientist, as distinct from the 'nocturnal' philosophy produced for them by philosophers (cf. RR, p. 44), is both realist in a way that Rorty finds objectionable, and intrinsic to the ongoing practice of the sciences themselves.

This has two aspects. Is science 'methodical' and is it 'realist'? Rorty denies, like Feyerabend, that there is such a thing as 'scientific method'. His main ground for this seems to be that there is no algorithm or formula for doing science. But can there not be non-algorithmic methods? Why should there not be interesting theoretical redescriptions of science? Why should science be uniquely exempt from theory, old and new?

Why not 'relax' here? Rorty operates a characteristic dilem-
matic disjunction here: *either* science is algorithmic *or* it is
unmethodical. We are offered a choice between a rigid fundamentalist demand and a soft deflationary option. This is
typical of Rorty; and it exemplifies the very 'Cartesian anxiety'
that Bernstein sees Rorty's work as exposing. This is that *either*
there is some basic foundational constraint *or* we are confronted with intellectual and moral chaos.[21] Bernstein goes on
to remark that Rorty succumbs to a version of it, viz. *either* we
are ineluctably tempted by foundational metaphors *or* we
must recognize that philosophy is at best a form of kibitzing.
Accuracy of representation is not the aim of science. *A fortiori*
descriptions of how science achieves that aim cannot be the
task of philosophy, which must thus become something else.

   But *science* can often explain the reliability of its own knowledge. Likewise, it can explain the shifting boundary between
the theoretical and the observable. And through, in Williams'
words, 'such achievements as evolutionary biology and the
findings of the neurological sciences' (AM, p. 31) it can make
an important 'contribution to explaining how science is itself
possible' (AM, p. 31) and 'how creatures which have the
origins and characteristics it says we have can understand the
properties it says the world has' (AM, pp. 30–1). As Williams
says, these features of science 'contribute, from within scientific reflection itself, to an image of the objects of science that
Rorty says we should not have; that is, to a conception of the
world as it is, independently of our enquiries' (AM, p. 31).
This is indeed the natural ontological attitude of the sciences.
And, in forbidding us to subscribe to it, Rorty tacitly reoccu-
pies the Archimedean standpoint – of a transcendent and
privileged observer – that he is enjoining us to reject. For, as
Williams puts it, 'if it is overwhelmingly convenient to say
that science describes what is already there, and if there are
no deep metaphysical or epistemological issues here but only
a question of what is convenient ... then what everyone
should be saying, including Rorty, is that science describes a
world already there'[22] – which is precisely what he urges us
not to say.

Metaphysically we can develop what I called the natural ontological attitude into the transcendental realist conception of a philosophically *Copernican–Darwinian world*, i.e. of a world in which the independently existing and transfactually active objects of our (present) knowledge, in time produced subjects who could come to know these objects, their subjectivity and this (Copernican–Darwinian) relation. But Rorty goes out of his way to admonish Sellars and Rosenberg for related views (see PMN, p. 297). He is now in an especially awkward corner for he still has to persuade us that his own kibitzing, his fossicking around in the history of philosophy, ironically joshing his contemporaries into light-minded playfulness – will have negligible or at least non-negative effects on science; that it can be conceived as a purely private matter – of his obsessions with philosophy's obsessions – which will have no deleterious effects, particularly on the underdeveloped and methodologically self-conscious human sciences.

NOTES

1 Cf. J. Habermas, *Knowledge and Human Interests*, London, 1972, p. 308. For some consequences of this see SR, pp. 230–1 n. 5; and RR, pp. 188–9.

2 Davidson's theory is elaborated in *Essays on Actions and Events*, Oxford, 1980, especially essays 1, 7 and 11. For a critique of it, see RTS, pp. 140–1.

3 Cf. 'A reply to Dreyfus and Taylor', *The Review of Metaphysics* 33 (1980), p. 45.

4 Thus, as we shall see in Part IV, there is another story to be told about 'reference', besides the one told by Rorty in PMN, chapter 6 (and elsewhere), albeit one whose most interesting line of development postdates PMN, namely as a story of the 'search and find' activities of scientists looking for and exploring the novel entities and structures posited in scientific theories. See e.g. I. Hacking, *Representing and Intervening*, Cambridge, 1983; and R. Harré, *Varieties of Realism*, Oxford, 1986. This type of story presupposes that science has distinctive procedures as well as determinate results, and that it is a material practice as

well as a theoretical discourse. Cf. also A. MacIntyre, 'Epistemological crises, dramatic narratives and the philosophy of science', *The Monist*, vol. 60 (1977), p. 459.

5 See A. Donagan, 'The Popper–Hempel theory reconsidered',
   Philosophical Analysis and History, ed. W. H. Dray, New York,
   1966.

6 See M. Scriven, 'Truisms as the grounds for historical explanations', *Theories of History*, ed. P. Gardiner, New York, 1963.

7 See my 'Introduction: realism and human being' to *Harré and his
   Critics*, ed. R. Bhaskar, Oxford, 1990.

8 See A. Chalmers, 'Bhaskar, Cartwright and realism in physics',
   Methodology and Science 20 (1987); and 'Is Bhaskar's realism
   realistic?', *Radical Philosophy* 49 (1988), plus my response in
   'Postscript to the second edition', PON 2, pp. 167–73.

9 Oxford, 1983.

10 W. Sellars, *Science, Perception and Reality*, London, 1963, p. 173,
   cited at PMN, p. 199. For more on the emergence of transcendental realism and its relationship to scientific, science-oriented
   and other realisms, see RR, chapter 9.

11 Cf. W. Outhwaite, *New Philosophies of Social Science*, London,
   1987, chapter 3.

12 See *The Structure of Scientific Revolutions*, 2nd edn, Chicago, 1970,
   p. 121. Cf. also: 'In a sense I am unable to explicate further, the
   proponents of competing paradigms practice their trades in
   different worlds', ibid., p. 150.

13 Rorty actually comes close to the difference between the two
   types of constitution (on which see SR, p. 105n; and W. Outhwaite, *Concept Formation in Social Science*, London, 1983, chapter 3) when he says that 'the relevant [i.e. epistemic] sense of
   "constitution" [must be] distinguished from the physical sense
   (in which houses are "constituted out of" bricks)' (ibid.) and
   that without the former 'fossils wouldn't be fossils, [but] merely
   rocks'. Of course, to say that an object is a rock requires interpretation, or at least classification, albeit pre-scientific, and
   hence a measure of epistemic constitution$_{td}$ too.

14 One strange manifestation of this in PMN may be briefly mentioned. Rorty seems to think it is possible to have a plurality of
   comprehensive closed theories of strictly Humean form: 'There
   are *lots* of vocabularies in the language within which one might
   expect to get a comprehensive theory phrased in homonomic
   generalisations, and science, political theory, literary criticism

and the rest will, God willing, continue to create more and more such vocabularies' (PMN, p. 208). He seems to be committed here to a most implausible species of what might be called a 'multiple aspect theory'. This position is especially odd because the motivation for the Davidsonian distinction between homonomic and heteronomic generalizations lies precisely in the absence of homonomic generalizations in such areas as political theory, literary criticism, the social sciences and psychology (and philosophy).

15 Rorty oscillates between three positions: (α) occasionally modelling literature upon science; (β) frequently modelling science upon literature; (γ) most characteristically contrasting science and literature. In general he adopts (α) for normal discourse, (β) for abnormal discourse and (γ) when concerned to debunk the pretensions of traditional (science-oriented) philosophy. His paradigm of science is normally that of instrumental or applied or proto-technological activity. Thus for the romantic philosopher, 'science is no more than the handmaiden of technology' (CIS, pp. 3–4).

16 Note the intransitive–transitive ambiguity implicit in the formulation: new things or old things made (by redescription) new?

17 It is also doubtful whether or not Rorty, as a 'strong textualist' or 'misreader' (CP, pp. 151–2) is or should be interested in the question of whether or not his is a correct as distinct from, say, an 'exciting', interpretation of Kuhn (cf. Rorty's treatment of Rawls in PDP).

18 Elsewhere (PMN, p. 372) enquiry is opposed to conversation.

19 'If the picture picture is as absurd as I think it is, it would be well that this absurdity should not become widely known. For the ironist poet owes far more to Parmenides and the tradition of Western metaphysics than does the scientist. The scientific culture could survive a loss of faith in this tradition, but the literary culture might not' (CP, p. 137). Is there not, then, a performative contradiction at the heart of Rorty's enterprise?

20 *Philosophical Investigations*, Oxford, 1963, I, §124.

21 See R. J. Bernstein, *Philosophical Profiles*, Cambridge, 1986, p. 42.

22 B. Williams, *Ethics and the Limits of Philosophy*, Glasgow, 1985, pp. 137–8.

2

Pragmatism, Epistemology and the Inexorability of Realism

The highest point reached by contemplative materialism, that is, materialism which does not comprehend sensuousness as practical activity, is the contemplation of single individuals and of civil society.
K. Marx, '9th Thesis on Feuerbach', *Early Writings*

The standpoint of the old materialism is civil society; the standpoint of the new is human society, or social humanity
K. Marx, '10th Thesis on Feuerbach', *Early Writings*

The principle of the existential intransitivity of objects, that things in general exist and act independently of their descriptions, must be complemented by the principle of the historical transitivity of knowledge, that we can only know those things under particular and potentially transformable descriptions (cf. RTS, p. 250; SR, p. 99). But it does not follow from the principle of the historical transitivity of knowledge that we cannot know that what is known (under particular descriptions) exists and acts independently of those descriptions. Rorty is correct that 'there is no inference from "one cannot give a theory-independent description of a thing" to "there are no theory-independent things"' (PMN, p. 279). But equally there is no inference from 'there is no way to know a thing except under a particular description' to 'there is no way to know that that thing exists (and acts) independently of its particular description (and descriptions in general)'. In fact, one can know that scientifically significant reality existed and acted prior to and independently of that relative latecomer science as a truth in (a result of) sciences (of cosmology and geogony, biology and anthropology), and one can know that it exists and acts independently of science as a practical pre-supposition of the social activity of science (and a truth in philosophy). Of course, what is known – in the discourse of philosophy – to exist and act independently of science will always be known in some more or less specific way – whether in the relatively Neanderthal forms of Peircian 'secondness' (PMN, p. 375) or Maine de Biran's 'intransigence'[1] or what Putnam has called '19th-century ... village atheism'[2] or in the form of a more fully elaborated ontology.

Such generic characterizations of the world can and do play a significant role in the practice of science; and some ontology, or general account of being, and hence some kind of realism, will in any event be implicitly presupposed, if it is not explicit-ly theorized, in a philosophical or indeed a first-order practical discourse on science. The crucial questions in philosophy are not whether to be a realist or an anti-realist, but *what sort* of realist to be (an empirical, conceptual, transcendental or whatever realist); whether one explicitly theorizes or merely implicitly secretes one's realism; and whether and how one decides, arrives at or absorbs one's realism. While arguing that we never encounter reality *except under a chosen description* (CP, p. xxxix), Rorty unwittingly imbibes and inherits Hume's and Kant's chosen descriptions of the reality known by the sciences.

Ontology is irreducible, partly because different (for in-stance, cognitively-oriented) practices presuppose different and incompatible accounts of the world. It is not sufficient to '[explain] rationality and epistemic authority by reference to what society lets us say' (PMN, p. 179) precisely because 'what society lets us say' can itself always be '[placed] in the logical space of reasons, of justifying [and, we must add, criticizing] and being able to justify [and criticize] what one says' (PMN, p. 182). That is to say, what society or one's peers and contemporaries *ought* to let one say is always a legitimate question, especially in the case of *conflicts*, actual or potential, between different language-games, as is chronically the case in the contested and quandarous human sciences.

We can also begin to appreciate why we need to sustain the concept of an ontological realm distinct from our current claims to knowledge of it. First, for the intelligibility of their establishment, involving, as they do, creative redescription of, and active intervention in, nature. Second, for the possibility of their criticism and rational change (see RTS, p. 43). (I shall deal with Rorty's claim that the transitions between normal discourses, paradigms or language-games, though caused, cannot be reasoned (CC, pp. 10–11; CIS, pp. 49–50) below.) Rorty's 'transcendentalia' (PMN, pp. 310–11) now become, from this perspective, necessary features of the immanent practices of the sciences. The fact that a truth claim characteristically expresses a claim about how the world is, *irrespective of how any particular agent or group believes (or wants) it to be*, both accounts for the gap between 'warrantedly assertible' and 'true' (PMN, pp. 280, 306) and, precisely as our homely and shopworn sense (PMN, p. 308), potentially and unconditionally opens up any given truth-claim to challenge from conflicting points of view.[3] Furthermore, even Rorty's welcome warnings about the dangers of reifying or hypostatizing truth become misleading (and ecologically irresponsible) if they are taken to imply that there are no real-world constraints on beliefs or to license a poetic or practical Prometheanism to the effect that there are 'no non-human forces to which human beings should be responsible' (CC, p. 10; CIS, p. 48).

I now want to isolate and comment on five pivotal presuppositions of Rorty's work. Rorty assumes that:

1 Science can get by without philosophy, and in particular metaphysics and ontology.
2 Any (philosophical) realism must be a truth-realism.

3 The only kind of realism science needs is what Putnam calls an 'internal realism' (PMN, pp. 281, 341) – which is required for purposes of Whiggish historiography.

4 The Humean theory of causal laws (at least as modified by Davidson) and the deductive–nomological accounts of explanation and prediction (and *a fortiori* their symmetry) are in order and correct.

5 Their truth is compatible with the possibility of the *Geisteswissenschaften* and in particular the *wirkungsgeschichtliches Bewusstsein* (or historically effective consciousness) (PMN, p. 359), central to the projects of 'edification' and emancipatory social science alike.

None of these assumptions withstands critical scrutiny.

Rorty takes over Kant's conflation of the *a priori* and the subjective (criticized in SR, pp. 11ff.) (see PMN, pp. 8–9, 258) and thus sees the only possible locus of necessity as 'within the mind' (PMN, p. 189). He thus assumes that any transcendental philosophy is going to be primarily epistemological or epistemologically-oriented (PMN, p. 381). This prematurely forecloses the possibility of a philosophy of or for science, which was no longer concerned to 'ground' knowledge or find certain foundations for it; but which was instead concerned to ask what the *world* must be like for certain characteristic (practical and discursive) social activities of science to be possible.[4] Such a philosophy would be a transcendental realism, not idealism; ontologically, rather than epistemologically, geared; and unafraid of recognizing epistemically relativist implications – which are, as already mentioned, quite consistent with judgementally rationalist results (PON 1, pp. 73–4; PON 2, pp. 57–8).

From such a philosophical perspective, reality can be unequivocally (and no longer anthropocentrically or epistemologically) accorded to things. It would be wrong to cleave, for instance, to the slogan that 'to be is to be the value of a variable'.[5] For the way things are in the world takes no particular account of how humans are, or whether and how they choose to represent them. Moreover, from such a perspective, (natural) necessity would, like reality, when appropriate, be unequivocally ascribed to the efficacy of causal laws and generative mechanisms and to the existence of some properties of structures and things (RTS, chapter 3.3 and 3.5). It would reflect a superstitious anthropomorphism to believe that 'necessity resides in the way we say things, and not in the things we talk about'.[6] Also, from such a perspective, there would remain no temptation to identify or treat as synonyms the 'ontological' and the 'empirical' (see PMN, p. 188). For such a philosophy would have a use for the category of the 'non-empirical but real', for example, in designating the transfactual operation of causal laws prior to, outside and independently of human experience.

Finally, such a transcendental philosophy would unashamedly acknowledge as a corollary of its realism, the historicity, relativity and essential transformability of all our knowledge. Putnam's 'disastrous meta-induction'[7] loses its force if one no longer conflates ontological realism and epistemological absolutism and thinks of absolutism and irrationalism as the only alternatives, thereby rejecting the Rortian–Cartesian disjunct discussed on p. 20 above. Indeed, from this standpoint Putnam's induction should be welcomed – as underscoring the historicity, fallibility and potential transformability of all our cognitive (as other) achievements (cf. PON 2, pp. 170–1; RR, pp. 183–4). Rorty avoids the 'relativist predicament' (CC, p. 11; CIS, p. 50) only by the twin expedients of deploying an epistemic absolutism for normal science and an epistemic irrationalism for abnormal science, or more generally discourse. In the former case he invokes Davidson's arguments against alternative conceptual schemes and assumes that within a language-game or discourse 'everybody agrees on how to evaluate everything everybody else says' (PMN, p. 320). In the latter case he stipulates that what is believed or said, though, like Davidsonian metaphors (CC, p. 14; CIS, p. 36), caused, cannot be reasoned, so that 'the most human beings can do is to manipulate the tensions within their own epoch in order to produce the beginnings of the next epoch' (CC, p. 11; CIS, p. 50). This is a counsel of despair. It stems partly from the over-normalization of normal discourse, ignoring its holes, silences and incommensurabilities, its ambiguities and ambivalences, its open texture and rich potentialities for development, and also the fact that developing traditions are typically characterized by rival or conflicting interpretations.[8] Partly too from the failure to allow anything like immanent critique (including the possibility of metacritique (RR, p. 98; SR, pp. 25–6)) as a process of rational disputation and change in the synchronic and diachronic space or overlap between language-games, where all the interesting (and truly dialectical) arguments take place and develop, and without which there would be nothing very much, if at all, to say (see PON 1, p. 190; PON 2, p. 148). In a way nothing is more significant for understanding the political (in a broad sense) impact of Rortyism as a phenomenon than the implications of the doctrine that revolutionary change (whether in the sciences, the arts or the socio-economic–political world generally) cannot be rational.

To sum up on point (1) above, then, we can affirm that there is no Archimedean point outside human history and no 'third thing' – no 'tertium' – called correspondence standing between language and the world. But this does not mean that we do not need a philosophical de-divinized (and de-anthropomorphized) ontology, in which to think (a) the contingency of our origins, of human experience and human reason (and hence the possibility of an unexperienced or an a-rational(ized) world); (b) the finitude of human being (including the uncompleted or unfinished character of human lives); and (c) the historicity of human knowledge (within what I have called the transitive dimension in the philosophy of science).

Contrary to (2) above, I suggest that what is required to underlabour for science is not an epistemologically slanted truth realism of the sort that the pre-1976 Putnam and the tradition have sought to provide, but an ontologically primed causal powers and tendencies of things realism of the kind that I sketched in RTS and Harré and Madden elaborated in *Causal Powers*.[9]

As regards (3), there are places (for instance, at PMN, pp. 282 and 341) where the type of internal realist historiography, which Rorty reckons a sufficient realism, might appear to differ little from the account a transcendental realist would provide. But there are differences in metaphysics, ideological intent and rhetorical style. The transcendental realist is un-blushingly fallibilist and historicist about science. She feels no need to be uncritical and 'complimentary' about everything that passes for knowledge or is done in science's name (cf. PMN, p. 298); no reason to 'buy in' to shoddy science (see RTS, p. 188); no compunction about admitting to occasional (and even persistent) intra-scientific perplexity or 'stuckness'. Nor does she feel under any imperative to write the history of science Whiggishly as one long, continuous success story – without blemishes or periods of stasis or moments of pratfall and even regression. For she never forgets that science is something that human beings have made, in causal interac-tion with the things they have found, in nature.

As for (4), we have already seen that Humean and Hempe-lian theory are inconsistent with the practical activity and substantive content of science. (5) will be considered in Part II of this study.

It is true that nature has no preferred way of being represented;[10] that 'nature speaks being', like the Heideg-gerian 'language speaks man' (CC, p. 11; CIS, p. 50), is only a metaphor. But the following should be borne in mind. In spite of the indisputable formal underdetermination of theory by evidence, at any moment of time in most scientific domains for most of the time, there will be only one or two plausible theories consistent with the data and/or revealing promise as potentially fruitful research lines. Theories are islands in 'oceans of anomalies' (cf. RR, p. 31). Secondly, in what might be called the 'epistemic stance' to nature,[11] we do tend to 'read' the world, as we read the time off a clock or the sentences off a page, as if it were constituted by facts, i.e. under the descriptions of a theory (see SR, chapter 3.6). And in this stance it is even reasonable to talk of one rather than another vocabulary as (contra CIS, p. 5) improving the legibility of nature. Further, to say that theory conditions our beliefs in epistemically significant perception is not to say that theory determines them. Theory and nature may be co-determinants of beliefs in a notional parallelogram of forces (see SR, pp. 189–91), and we may appeal to either (in propositionalized form) in a justificatory context. (In fact, Rorty allows for the control of theory by observation in the guise of 'control by less controversial over more controversial beliefs' (PMN, pp. 275–6n). But beliefs of the former kind may be less controversial precisely because they were acquired in or as a result of (theoretically informed) observation.) Finally, we must never forget the immense effort that goes into that nitty-gritty practical laboratory activity, which Bacon called 'twisting the lion's tail',[12] designed precisely to create or induce conditions under which grounds for a theoretical judgement will become possible. Such practical activity, comprising social transactions between human beings and their material transactions with nature, constitutes the woof and warp of getting into 'the logical space of reasons, of justifying and being able to justify what one says' (PMN, p. 182), the staple diet of normal science.

What is the epistemological problematic, which Rorty identifies and partially describes, but in which, in my view, he remains entrapped? For Rorty, it is a problem-field, which is also a project or quest and a theory or solution-set. The project is to identify certain foundations for knowledge, which philosophy purports to do on the basis of its special understanding of the nature of knowledge or mind. The Cartesian–Lockean–Kantian tradition has conceived philosophy as foundational, knowledge as representational and the mental as privileged and even incorrigible. At the core of philosophy has been the quest for certainty, in response to the possibility of Cartesian (sceptical) doubt. This, in its dominant empiricist form, it has found in the immediate deliverances of sense (rather than, or sometimes as well as, in self-evident truths of reason – or their analytical proxies, such as meanings).

Rorty's sustained polemic against foundationalism in PMN

(and elsewhere) is accompanied by a vigorous assault on its attendant ocular metaphors, mirror imagery and overseer conception of philosophy. Most of this I wholeheartedly endorse. In PMN he isolates one particular moment in the genesis of foundationalist epistemology of special importance. This is what I call the 'ontic fallacy' (SR, p. 23). It consists in the effective ontologization or naturalization of knowledge, the reduction of knowledge to, or its determination by, being in what may best be regarded as a species of *compulsive belief-formation* (see PMN, pp. 158, 374–7). (Thus Plato focused on 'the various parts of the soul and of the body being compelled in their respective ways by their respective objects' (PMN, p. 158).) Rorty sees that this involves the dehumanization of discursive, justifying subjects, and the collapse, in the alleged moment of cognition, of the *pour-soi* to the *en-soi*, of justification to para-mechanical explanation. ('It is the notion of having reality unveiled to us ... with some unimaginable sort of immediacy which would make discourse and description superfluous' (PMN, p. 375).[13]) But – and this is one sense in which PMN is based on a half-truth – Rorty does not recognize that it is the epistemic dual or counterpart of the ontic fallacy, namely the humanization of nature, in an anthropomorphic, epistemological definition of being (in empiricism, in terms of the concept of experience) in the *epistemic fallacy*, which prepares the way and paves the ground for the ontologization (eternalization and divinization) of knowledge in a subject–object identity or correspondence theory. Such a theory effectively welds together the transitive or social-epistemic and the intransitive or ontic dimensions of science (see SR, pp. 66, 253). On it knowledge is naturalized and being epistemologized.

It is to the compulsive belief-formation involved in the ontic fallacy that, as we shall see, Rorty *voluntaristically* overreacts in his concept of effectively *unconstrained belief-formation*. His neglect of the epistemic fallacy is of a piece with the philosophical tradition. Transcendental or critical realism, by contrast, starting its analysis from within human being (and achievements such as knowledge) shows how this being has as its

condition something not-human being at all (e.g. transfactually efficacious causal laws in a structured, differentiated
and changing 'external' world). It thus embraces a critique of
all anthropomorphisms and anthropocentrisms, and what
could be called the *anthropomorphic fallacy* – the definition or
analysis of being in terms of human being – of which the
epistemic fallacy is an instance. Incidentally, if Rorty were
to be serious about and consistent with his rhetoric
of de-divinization, then he should welcome the de-
anthropomorphization or de-humanization of nature as a step
– the crucial step – on the road to de-divinization.

The above-mentioned problematic, which may fairly be
called 'epistemological', has ontological and social conditions
and consequences. The drive to certainty, powered by
epistemology's sceptical foil, sets up a dialectic in which
correspondence must give way to, or be philosophically
underpinned by, identity. Similarly, accuracy of representation must pass over into immediacy of content. Thus, in its
dominant empiricist form, the objects intuited in experience
and their constant conjunctions come, in the ideology of
empirical realism, to define the world, stamp being in a Humean mould. The sociological precondition of the atomistic
and uniform ontology of empirical realism is an individualism,
comprised of autonomized units, conjoined (if at all) by con-
tract, passive recipients of a given and self-evident world
rather than active agents in a complex, structured and developing one. For such isolated consciousnesses, disengaged
from material practice, their relations to their bodies, other
minds, external objects and even their own past selves must
become doubtful (cf. RR, p. 128). Philosophy's task – that of
the traditional 'problems of philosophy' – now becomes to
reconstruct and indemnify our actual knowledge in a way
congruent with these conceptions of man and being (cf. PON
1, p. 10; PON 2, p. 8).

What explains this problematic? There seems little doubt
about the role of the fundamentalist exercise. It is surely, as
Rorty suggests, a misguided attempt to eternalize the normal
discourse of the day (PMN, pp. 9–10, 333n). Moreover, it is

philosophy's fundamentalist ambitions that justify the ontology. This ontology, formulated in the antiquated vocabulary of Newtonian and Humean mechanics, is now seriously 'interfering with' (CL, p. 5; CIS, p. 12) our efforts to investigate and change the social world. What explains *it*? Could it be anything other than the conception of man – of single individuals in civil society – at the heart of it? Perhaps the real meaning of the epistemological project is not epistemological at all, but ontological: to reconstitute the (known) world in the self-image of bourgeois man.

If this, or something like it, is part of the meaning of the epistemological tradition, which has come down to us from Descartes and Locke through Hume and Kant and their descendants, what should be said about the role of epistemology within the context of the transcendental realist philosophy I have been advocating here? We can appreciate the need for *some*, if you like, counter-traditional or even anti-epistemological epistemology by reflecting on the irreducible normativity of social practices which Rorty notes (PMN, p. 180n). This begins to show us why, from the standpoint of what I have called the 'axiological imperative', namely the condition that we must act (and other than by scrutinizing the antecedents of what we will do) (PON 1, p. 111; PON 2, p. 87), we need an intrinsic (intentional, justifying) as well as (and, when it is efficacious, within the context of) the extrinsic (historical, explaining) aspect of science (see SR, pp. 16ff).

I think that, despite his polemics against epistemology (as normally understood)[14] *per se*, Rorty half-concedes this point when talking of the 'bifocality' of science:

> From the point of view of the group in question these subjective conditions are a combination of commonsensical practical imperatives (e.g. tribal taboos, Mill's Methods) with the standard current theory about the subject.[15] From the point of view of the historian of ideas or the anthropologist they are the empirical facts about the beliefs, desires and practices of a certain group of human beings. These are incompatible points of view, in the sense that we cannot be at both viewpoints simultaneously. (PMN, p. 385)

An epistemology or criteriology for science is required just in so far as science is an irreducibly normative social activity, oriented to specific aims (in theory, the structural explanation of manifest phenomena) and characterized by specific methods of its own (see RTS, chapter 3).

Now if value judgements of one sort or another are irreducible in the sciences, does this mean that they neither require nor receive grounds other than the agreement of one's peers (see PMN, p. 176)? Certainly not. For, in the first place, a value judgement, including one of truth, typically incorporates a descriptive or evidential component alongside its prescriptive, imperatival or practical component (see SR, p. 183). To ignore the former, the descriptive ('factual' or ontological) grounds in virtue of which some belief or action is commended and recommended, could be called the emotivist or more generally *anti-naturalistic fallacy* in axiology. But can such grounds be cashed in any way other than by reference to what some community believes about the world? Most certainly.

Outside science, a belief or action may be justified (or criticized) by reference to what the (relevant) scientific community believes. But generally *inside* (the relevant part of) science, we cannot justify, say, an explanatory claim in this way. This may be partly because what is at stake (what stands in need of justification or criticism) is precisely what the community believes. But it will also be in part because at some point the explanatory query *in* science will take the form 'why is the world this way?', whereas the explanatory query *about* science will take the form 'why does this community believe such-and-such?'. The answer to the former question will not consist of intellectual–cultural history or the natural sociology of belief (SR, p. 189), but of a (scientifically-) ontologically grounded, or justified, scientific explanation.

Intra-scientific justifications (in the intrinsic aspect of science) will appeal to formal proofs, plausible models, decisive experiments, reliable apparatus, newly discovered phenomena, consistency with established theory, and so forth. (It is true that they will also appeal to trustworthy, good, sound observers, experimentalists, designers, etc.,[16] but these too must be explicated as *grounds for*, not, or not merely, as causes of, belief in the explanation or whatever.) Together, they will amount to a justification, couched in terms of some substantive scientific ontology, of the explanation offered of the puzzling phenomenon, rather than a sociological explanation (in the extrinsic aspect of science) of that community's (or person's) belief. To confound the two would be to commit all over again a transposed variant of the Lockean mistake of confusing justification and explanation, which Rorty mercilessly exposes in PMN, chapter 3.

Of course, justifications within science are a social matter – but they require and are given ontological grounds. In failing to recognize this, Rorty has furnished us with a post-epistemological theory of knowledge without justification. This matches his account of science without being.[17] The result is just the opposite of what he intended: the epistemologization of being and the incorrigibility (uncriticizability) of what passes for knowledge.

I argued above for the irreducibility of 'why is the world this way?' questions to 'why does this (my, your, their, that) community believe such-and-such?' questions. A pragmatist of Rortian stripe might accept this, but then go on to contend that 'why is the world this way?', or more generally 'what is so?' questions are reducible to the question 'what is it best for me to believe?', or more simply 'what shall I believe?'. Such a pragmatist would question not so much the need for an intrinsic aspect as that for an intransitive dimension of science. He would be of individualist–existentialist *voluntarist* rather than collectivist–conventionalist conformist temper; and he would want to see all theoretical questions about how, why and what the world is as species of *practical* questions about the benefit or utility of beliefs. *Prima facie* this is not a plausible position. If my believing x minimizes my pain, is this a reason for believing x unless it is also the case that x is true? Even if it is, we may sometimes have to choose between happiness (utility and/or well-being) and truth. This shows that the concepts are distinct. The truth can hurt.

Nevertheless, central to pragmatism seems the notion that at least some – perhaps large-scale – beliefs can, must and should be chosen, and chosen on practical grounds. Thus Rorty says: 'When the contemplative mind ... takes large views its activity is more like deciding what to *do* than deciding that a representation is accurate' (CP, p. 163). And in a passage already discussed (CIS, p. 5, p. 14 above), Rorty explicitly differentiates individual sentences where the world 'contains the causes of our being justified in holding a belief' (sic) with the choice of vocabularies, paradigms or language-games as a whole where 'the idea that the world decides which descriptions are true can no longer be given a clear sense'. It is as if we were free to choose vocabularies but, once chosen, determined within them by the way the world is. Indeed, there is much to be said, as we shall see, for the interpretation of Rorty as a micro-positivist and a macro-pragmatist. But now we have to ask whether an ontologically unconstrained axiology is possible, or even intelligible, at any level. It seems clear that it is not. As Jane Heal puts it,

> the idea that we can abandon 'what is so?' questions in favour of 'what shall I believe?' questions is absurd. Our notion of action is of something which operates under certain constraints which we do not place there but, in some sense, find. The question of what these constraints are, questions of [the] form 'what is so?' must present themselves to any creature who is also asking questions [of the type 'what shall I do?', 'what shall I intend?' and 'what shall I believe?'] in any manner comprehensible to us. And the asking of questions of the form 'what is so?' presupposes that the questioner *may* find an answer *given* to him.... We cannot get away from the idea of *finding* things to be so, *having it borne in on us* that they are and the like. (AM, p. 111)

A creature whose belief-formation was unconstrained would be a (Kantian) archetypal understanding for whom no distinction between thinking and doing and no concept of grounds or evidence would be possible. On the contrary, rational action in our world presupposes constraints and rational belief evidence. In particular, we are not free to believe what we choose if we are to attain the sort of objectives Rorty mentions in his books: freedom from the scarcity of food and the secret police (PMN, p. 359), or the reduction of suffering, and especially cruelty, and the achievement of private perfection (CIS, passim).

It seems likely that Rorty's unconstrained belief-formation is a voluntaristic reaction to the compulsive belief-formation encapsulated in the ontic fallacy. But one can have real-world constraints on theory choice and development without these constraints compulsively determining them. Once more one misses in Rorty any theory of justification (criticism and critique). The result is a macro-'super-idealist' epistemology, in which discourse is effectively unconstrained by extra-discursive reality (see RR, chapter 2), erected – in the guise of an undifferentiated linguistic monism – as a Nietzschean–Kuhnian superstructure – on a Humean–Hempelian micro-ontological base.

But voluntarism – often combined with individualism – is a persistent feature of Rorty's more recent work, functioning to generate a contrast with the inert merely found. Thus human beings do not 'make languages' (CIS, p. 9). They find them ready-made at birth. And in acquiring and using them they reproduce and, to an extent, transform them. Institutions are not normally 'invented' *de novo*; rather, they develop from what pre-exists them. They may occasionally have 'founders' and 'preservers', but for the most part their production, reproduction and transformation occur in a tacit, unconscious way. Nor is a society best conceived 'as a band of eccentrics collaborating for purposes of mutual protection' (CIS, p. 59).[18] Rorty has very little sense of the depth and opacity of social structures. And this shows up in his discussion of belief. At CIS, p. 179, Rorty says: 'Although we can say "I believed something false", nobody can say to himself "I am, right now, believing something false".' But such a position completely overlooks the stratification and complexity of beliefs and the sort of phenomena (which Rorty touches on in FMR) most clearly caught in the concepts of psychological rationalization and ideological mystification (SR, chapter 2.6–7),[19] but also exemplified by everyday talk about unconscious, unarticulated, underlying, pathological (neurotic, obsessive, etc.), contradictory, sticky and recalcitrant beliefs. In cases of complex belief-forms, we may well have to ask how and why I or some other agent came to hold their current erroneous beliefs. Indeed, I have argued elsewhere that the possibility of such a depth-investigation (which logically embraces the first-person case) is both implicit in the programme of the sociology of knowledge and a presupposition of any rational discourse or authentic act of self-reflection (PON, 1, p. 82; PON 2, p. 64). In assuming the transparency and malleability of beliefs – that we are free to believe what we will – Rorty also overlooks those cases of strategic belief formation where we have to employ a more or less devious route to believe something true but difficult or false but beneficial ('white lies', etc.).[20] But it should be stressed that to believe something knowingly false or irrespective of whether it is true or false (for the sake of some higher-order end) is a position we cannot normally or systematically be in (cf. SR, chapter 2.4).

The omission of an explicit intransitive dimension in Rorty comes across in a number of deleterious ways. Rorty claims: 'For us ironists, nothing can serve as a criticism of a final vocabulary save another such vocabulary; there is no answer to a redescription save a re-re-redescription' (CIS, p. 80). First, the notion of a final vocabulary is suspect. Rorty introduces it by saying: 'All human beings carry about a set of words which they employ to justify their actions, their beliefs and their lives ... I shall call these words a person's "final vocabulary".... It is final in the sense that if doubt is cast on the worth of these words, their user has no non-circular argumentative recourse' (CIS, p. 78). But this overlooks the penumbra of such words ('decency', 'England', 'cricket', etc.) – their inexplicitness and the multiply-threaded, adaptably shifting and open-textured nature of such 'vocabularies' in real life; as well as the possibilities of immanent criticism, or criticism from one part of a vocabulary to another part, or criticism which is empirical and piecemeal (justification is not

unilinear) or which comes from an internally related but conflicting tradition. Rorty himself in his work is always finding
ways of getting round stand-offs (cf. CIS p. 51). It is only
rarely, if ever, that we have to say: 'I have reached bedrock
and my spade is turned.'[21]

Secondly, the intelligibility of redescription (in the transitive
dimension) normally involves a realm of objects (in the intransitive dimension), which are the objects of the redescription.
In lopping off the intransitive domain, Rorty forgets that texts
normally stand in relation not only to other texts, but to
things, and that such things – referents – may include texts,
poems and conversations. Moreover, the redescription may
conform to perfectly rational criteria – such as greater explanatory power, predictive accuracy under closure, number of
problems solved, etc. Further, even when the subject-change
(or Kuhn-loss (SR, pp. 80–1)) is total and there is no topical
continuity, there will be normally be conversational – transitive – constraints on change. In any event, whether or not
these constraints are waived, it is not that there is now no
referent, but that the referent (in the intransitive dimension)
has completely changed.

Thirdly, associated with Rorty's transitivization of science
and culture goes a fondness for a metaphor for scientific and
cultural change as horizontal redescription rather than vertical
deepening (CP, p. 92; CIS, p. 96). This is a quite bogus
contrast. As we get to know more about some newly identified structures ('vertically'), we will often need to revise our
descriptions of familiar ones ('horizontally'). Conversely, falsification of old descriptions will often harbinger or necessitate
new discoveries. Next, Rorty's desire to avoid anything
approximating to real-world reference takes him close to self-
referential paradox: 'The difficulty faced by a philosopher . . .
like myself . . . – one who thinks of himself as auxiliary to the
poet rather than the physicist – is to avoid hinting that this
suggestion gets something right, that my sort of philosophy
corresponds to the way things really are' (CIS, p. 7). But it is
extremely difficult to take Rorty any other way. Would Rorty

really be unruffled by the suggestion that he grievously misinterprets Proust in CIS?[22]

Rorty's deontologized super-idealist epistemology involves an attack on the idea that the world has an intrinsic nature. 'Only if we have in mind ... some picture of the universe as either itself a person or as created by a person, can we make sense of the idea that the world has an intrinsic nature' (CL, p. 6; CIS, p. 21). Now I have argued that Rorty's own subscription to the epistemic fallacy tacitly personalizes the world, in defining the world as empirical, essentially experiencable by persons. Rorty goes on to remark that the idea that science reveals the world's intrinsic nature is one product of a general tendency 'to see the scientist (or the philosopher, or the poet, or *somebody*) as having a priestly function, as putting us in touch with a realm that transcends the human'. But I have tried to show that in philosophical ontology we need the concept of a realm of an identifiable sort (e.g. as structured, differentiated and changing), which transcends, but includes, the human precisely to avoid anthropomorphism and as a condition of the intelligibility of scientific life. Moreover, science itself makes use of the contrasts between (a) those properties of an object that comprise its intrinsic nature or real essence (e.g. the chemical composition of a crystal, the genetic code of a dog) and those that do not; and (b) those objects for which there is a significant use of the notion of their intrinsic nature and those (such as the group of persons whose surname begins with 'P' or the set of all actually existing tables) for which there is not (cf. RTS, pp. 209–10).

NOTES

1 See A. Kojève, *Introduction to the Reading of Hegel*, New York, 1969, p. 156.
2 *Meaning and the Moral Sciences*, London, 1978, p. 20.
3 Cf. T. McCarthy, 'Private irony and public decency: Richard Rorty's new pragmatism', *Critical Inquiry* 16, Winter 1990, especially p. 369.

4 Cf. W. Outhwaite, *New Philosophies of Social Science*, London, 1987, pp. 31–5.

5 W. V. O. Quine, 'Designation and existence', *Readings in Philosophical Analysis*, ed. H. Feigl and W. Sellars, New York, 1949, p. 50.

6 W. V. O. Quine, 'Three grades of modal involvement', *Ways of Paradox*, New York, 1966, p. 174.

7 See his *Meaning and the Moral Sciences*, p. 25. It is discussed at PMN, pp. 284ff.

8 Cf. A. MacIntyre, *After Virtue*, London, 1981, p. 206: 'Moreover when a tradition is in good order it is always partially constituted by an argument about the goods the pursuit of which gives that tradition its particular point and purpose.'

9 Blackwell, Oxford, 1975. See also A. Sayer, *Method in Social Science: A Realist Approach*, London, 1984; and A. Collier, *An Introduction to Critical Realism* (forthcoming).

10 But this is because nature has no preferences, not because it has no – and better and worse – representations.

11 For instance, in what F. Dretske, *Seeing and Knowing*, London, 1969, chapter 1 has called 'epistemic perception'.

12 There is some retrospective irony in this in view of Wittgenstein's famous aphorism about lions' talk: 'If a lion could talk, we could not understand him', *Philosophical Investigations*, II (xi), Oxford, 1963, p. 223.

13 'If we could convert knowledge from something discursive, something attained by continual adjustment of ideas or words, into something as ineluctable as being shoved about, or being transfixed by a sight which leaves us speechless, then we should no longer have the responsibility for choice among competing ideas and words, theories and vacabularies' (PMN, pp. 375–6).

14 Rorty sometimes – especially in Part 3 of PMN – uses a special sense of it (discussed in Part II below), on which it is counterposed to hermeneutics.

15 N.B. (1) The reduction of methodology to common sense, and (2) the tacit assumption that Mill's Methods, which presuppose a complete description of all the circumstances relevant to the outcome, are kosher.

16 Cf. B. Latour and S. Woolgar, *Laboratory Life*, Los Angeles, 1979.

17 Cf. 'the word "Being" is just more trouble than it is worth. I would be happy if Heidegger had never employed it', R. Rorty,

'Pragmatism without method', in *Sidney Hook: Philosopher of Democracy and Humanism*, ed. P. Kurtz, Buffalo, 1983, p. 267.

18 Or as 'a band of spirits united by a common goal' (CIS, p. 59).
19 For Rorty ideology means nothing more than 'bad idea' (CIS, p. 84n). By contrast see PON 'Appendix to chapter 2' and SR, chapter 3.2 §§ II and III.
20 Cf. B. A. O. Williams, 'Deciding to believe', *Problems of the Self*, Cambridge, 1973.
21 Wittgenstein, *Philosophical Investigations* I, § 217.
22 See B. Williams, 'Getting it right', *London Review of Books*, 23 November 1989, p. 5; or J. Bell, 'A liberal Utopia', *Times Literary Supplement*, 24 November 1989, p. 1296.

Part II

Agency

3

The Essential Tension of *Philosophy and the Mirror of Nature* – or a Tale of Two Rortys

Reason would overstep all its limits if it took upon itself to explain how pure reason can be practical. This would be identical with the task of explaining how freedom is possible.
                    I. Kant, *Grundlegung zur Metaphysik der Sitten*
                                              [*The Moral Law*]

A pervasive tension runs through PMN between (α) a hard-boiled scientistic naturalism of a physicalistic determinist cast, prominent to the fore, and (β) an acceptance of the autonomy of the *Geisteswissenschaften* and espousal of hermeneutics, accentuated towards the aft. Indeed, the book is a veritable tale of two Rortys – tough-minded Humean versus tender-minded existentialist. Rorty's subsequent trajectory has further tautened the tension – the actualism of PMN culminating in the apotheosis of contingency in the 1986 Northcliffe Lectures (henceforth NL) (published as CL, CS and CC) and the first part of CIS. Rorty is aware of the tension in PMN. So it is good to have his views on the apparent (and, I shall argue, real) incompatibility set out in two series of pithy paragraphs (on pp. 354–5 and 387–9), which I shall examine seriatim. For I want to claim that Rorty is unable to sustain either (1) an intelligible account of scientific activity (which involves, *inter alia*, causal intervention in nature to win 'epistemic access' to transfactually efficacious laws), or (2) an intelligible account of the world known by science, or (3) an adequate idea of human freedom, or (4) the compatibility between (α) and (β).

'Physicalism is probably right in saying that we shall someday be able, "in principle", to predict every movement of a person's body (including those of his larynx and his writing hand) by reference to microstructures within his body' (PMN, p. 354; cf. PMN, pp. 28n, 304–5, 387). Against this I am going to argue that a person's neurophysiology, or more generally physical microstructure, cannot constitute a closed system. This can be seen most easily by considering social interaction of an everyday sort. Suppose A goes into a newsagent's and says to the proprietor B, 'The *Guardian*, please', and B hands him a copy of it. On the physicalist thesis we must suppose that for any physical movement there is a set of antecedent (neurophysiological, or microstructural) states sufficient for it. Call B's action 'ϕB_1'. We must now suppose either (1) that ϕB_1 is determined by some set of antecedent physical states $N_0 \ldots N_n$ such that ϕB_1 would have been performed without A's speech action, ϕA_1; or (2) that A's speech action, ϕA_1, as understood by B, was causally efficacious in bringing out ϕB_1.

(1) involves the supposition that B would have performed the action of handing A a copy of the *Guardian*, ϕB_1, or the movements in which it physically consists, even if A had performed some quite different action, such as asking for the *Independent* or for a packet of chewing gum or B to marry him or dancing a jig, and even if A had not been present at all. This is absurd. But (2) involves an action of A's, as understood by B, intervening in the allegedly closed circuit constituted by B's neurophysiology (or microstructure). That is to say, it involves A's speech act as part of a causal sequence between some prior set of neurophysiological states of B and ϕB_1 – just as ϕB_1 intervenes between A's contemporaneous physical states and his subsequent action, ϕA_2, of giving B 40p. (We cannot suppose that A's movement would have occurred if B had said, 'Sorry, sold out', or passed him a copy

of the *Sun* or slapped his face or ignored him.) So B's (and A's) neurophysiology (or microstructure) cannot constitute a closed system. Thus in the context of social interaction, a person's body cannot be a closed system (cf. PON 1, pp. 133–6; PON 2, pp. 104–6).

This argument may be extended to cover the broader cases of open systemic agency generally, animal behaviour[1] and emergent natural powers. Here I consider only the first. Suppose C takes a stroll. It starts to rain. So she opens her umbrella. We must now suppose either (1') that C would have done so even if it had remained fine or (2') that the allegedly deterministic chain of neurophysiological (or microstructural) states is broken – in this case, by the weather.

There is a line of last resort that the reductionist might employ at (2), (2'), namely to deny that a single person's microstructure comprises a closed system. But now, physicalism loses its distinctiveness as a philosophical thesis applicable to *individual human beings* (see PMN, p. 387) and reduces merely to a barren form of Laplacean determinism, against which I have argued enough elsewhere (see RTS, especially chapter 2). What of (1), (1')? It might be maintained here that as a matter of fact ϕB_1 and only ϕB_1 will occur in response, so it appears, to ϕA_1; that given the state of B's microstructure nothing else could have occurred. What we are left with now is a bizarre variety of the Leibnizian pre-established harmony of monads, in which each person's microstructure is so synchronized with every other's that it appears *just as if* they were talking and dancing, batting and bowling, laughing and crying; and so synchronized with the microstructure of every other object in the universe that it appears *just as if* they were eating and drinking, building and digging, weaving and welding.

Only an emergent powers materialism, I want to claim, can sustain the phenomenon of agency (see PON, chapter 3.4–5; RTS chapter 2.5; and SR, chapter 2.1), and this entails a breakdown of the thesis of regularity determinism at the physical level. But we have already seen that the laws of nature, and the principles posited in scientific theories, cannot

be construed as constant conjunctions – i.e. they do not possess a closed systemic, regularity deterministic form. Rather,
they must be interpreted transfactually, as real tendencies
operating on and whatever (when their antecedent – stimulus
and releasing – conditions are satisfied) the flux of events.
Events, for their part, whether the fall of an autumn leaf, the
collapse of a bridge, the purchase of a newspaper, the composition of a poem or the decline of a civilization, are not
determined before they are caused (cf. RTS, p. 107).

Rorty's next paragraph begins: 'The danger to human freedom of such success is minimal, since the "in principle"
clause allows for the probability that the determination of the
initial conditions (the antecedent states of microstructures)
will be too difficult to carry out except as an occasional peda-
gogical exercise' (PMN, p. 354). This is disastrous. Freedom
cannot be grounded in ignorance. Or else we would have to
reckon a falling man free in virtue of his ignorance of gravity
or the law of fall. And the most free would be the least
pour-soi, the furthest from 'the logical space of reasons, of
justifying and being able to justify what one says' (PMN,
p. 389).

Rorty continues: 'The torturers and brainwashers are, in
any case, already in as good a position to interfere with human freedom as they would wish; further scientific progress
cannot improve their position.' Two brief comments. First,
torturers and brainwashers achieve their results by intervening in causal series, bringing about various physical effects
– including sounds, inscriptions, etc. – which, but for their
machinations, would not *ceteris paribus* (e.g. unless these
effects were overdetermined) have been forthcoming. Second,
the idea that technical progress could not improve their position seems to me like wishful thinking. It would be rash to
assume that subliminal advertising or market research were
wasted. The more the manipulators know about the immediate determinants of human action (CP), the more successful,
or so it would seem, they are likely to be.

Rorty's next paragraph may be broken down into:

1 'The intuition behind the traditional distinction between nature and spirit, and behind romanticism, is that we can predict what noises will come from someone's mouth without knowing what they mean.'
2 'Thus even if we could predict the sounds made by the community of scientific inquirers of the year 4000, we should not yet be in a position to join their conversation.'
3 'This intuition is quite correct.'

Proposition 2 is quite correct. If we *were* able to predict verbal behaviour, we still might not be able to know what the agents *meant*. Thus, as Winch has pointed out, we might be able to compute the statistical probability for the occurrence of certain sounds, e.g. words in Chinese, without being able to understand what was being said – and the converse is also the case (cf. PON 1, p. 175; PON 2, p. 137). But Rorty's intuition is faulty. For the reason why we cannot in general predict the sounds or inscriptions that people make unless we know what they mean to say is because it is the latter that determines the former. It is the state of the conversation, not physiology, which will explain the sounds and marks of the community of scientific enquirers for the year 4000, though these sounds and marks must be consistent with their physiology. Just as it is the state of the economy that determines the use of machines and thus selects the initial and boundary conditions under which certain mechanical principles apply. In human agency, the agent puts matter in motion, setting the conditions for the operation of various neurophysiological and physical laws, the outcome of which is not predetermined before it has actually been caused – by the agent in the context of her bio-psycho-social life. If the concept of human agency, as manifest in such phenomena as catching buses or writing poems, as distinct from mere bodily movement, as manifest in such phenomena as catching colds and digesting cakes, is to be sustained, it must be the case that the agent is causally responsible for some but not other of her bodily movements (cf. PON 1, p. 118; PON 2, p. 92).

I now have enough material to attempt a diagnosis of Rorty's reconciliation of the pervasive tension of PMN. It is a variant of Kant's resolution of the Third Antinomy. Now this does not work for Kant, and it does not work for Rorty. The problem for Kant is how we can be held responsible for the things we do, involving as they do bodily movements (including those of our larynxes and our writing hands), if all our physical movements are fully determined by antecedent physical causes. It is a problem for Rorty too. Kant has no answer to it – if we discount the idea of an original choice outside time (presumably an expedient not open to the naturalist Rorty). And whether we discount it or not, in either case, our ordinary system of causal imputation in the human world, and with it our moral accountancy, collapses.

What prevents an adequate resolution of the antinomy for Kant is his empirical realism, his thoroughgoing actualism and determinism, as detailed in the Analogies, to which he is wedded in his account of the phenomenal realm. For it is this that necessitates placing 'free man' in a realm, albeit one said to be possibly real (as distinct from merely apparent), outside and beyond the purchase of science. It is the ontology implicit in Kant's account of science, as manifest in his comprehensive actualism, that prevents him sustaining an adequate account of human causal agency, and a fortiori of freedom as a possible property or power of embodied agents in space and time.

Rorty comes to replicate the problematic of the Kantian solution. The basic distinction he invokes is that of Kant's ' "existentialist" distinction between people as empirical selves and as moral agents' (PMN, p. 382). We are determined as material bodies, qua empirical selves, but free as writing and speaking (i.e. discursive) subjects, qua moral agents. Actually, this is not quite as Rorty puts it, but I will justify the interpretation and elaboration in a moment. Whereas Kant gives us an (at least) two-worlds model, Rorty gives us an (at least) two-languages model. The autonomy of the social and other less physicalistic sciences is rendered consistent with the comprehensive empirical actualism by allowing that physics (or the physical sciences) can describe every bit of the phenomenal world, but that some (e.g. the human) bits of it can also be truly redescribed in a non-physicalistic way (PMN, pp. 28n, 205, 354, 387).

The problem for Rorty, as for Kant, is how, if the lower-order level is completely determined, what is described in higher-order terms can have any effect on it. And of course, the fact is that it cannot. If the intentional level, at which we cite reasons for actions and offer justifications and criticisms of beliefs, is merely a redescription of movements which are already sufficiently determined by antecedent physicalistic causes, then the *causal irrelevance of reasons* for the states of the phenomenal world of bodily movements and physical happenings (including the production of sounds and marks) immediately follows. Given this, both the particular reasons adduced in explanations, and the status of reason explanations in general, appear as arbitrary and the practices (from the Heideggerian *andenkendes Denken* (thinking that recalls) (CIS, p. 118) and the Gadamerian *wirkungsgeschichtliches Bewusstsein* (historically effective consciousness) (PMN, p. 359) of edification to the creative redescriptions of strong poets (CS, pp. 11ff; CIS pp. 24ff) or misreaders (CP, p. 151)) upon which they are based as illusory (cf. PON 1, pp. 112–14; PON 2, pp. 88–9).

Here again, as in Kant, it is Rorty's thoroughgoing actualism, determinism and deductivism that prevent an adequate account of embodied human agency, and *a fortiori* responsibility and freedom. There is a further difference here in that the relation between reality and appearance is inverted. In Kant the phenomenal world is merely apparent, but the noumenal world is real, which is what makes freedom possible. In Rorty, on the other hand, the phenomenal actualistically described world must be taken as real, with freedom dependent on our ignorance of (or decision to hold in abeyance) those deterministic descriptions of it. But the structure of the problem-field is the same. In both cases, reason explanations become arbitrary, and the only way to change the material world is by operating on sub-social (physical) causes. Science becomes unintelligible, social science impossible and freedom unattainable rationally.

It can be fairly commented that, having distinguished nine 'marks of the mental' early in PMN (p. 35), Rorty does not put himself to much trouble in dealing with the 'items bearing on personhood' (as distinct from reason and consciousness), viz. the ability to act freely; the ability to form part of our social group, to be 'one of us'; and the inability to be identified with any object 'in the world'.[3] The final place where he touches on these is in the second set of pithy paragraphs where he deals with the reconciliation of (α) and (β). Here he says we can assert all of the following:

1 Every speech, thought, theory, poem, composition and philosophy will turn out to be completely predictable in purely naturalistic terms. Some atoms-and-the-void account of micro-processes within individual human beings will permit the prediction of every sound or inscription which will ever be uttered. There are no ghosts.

2 Nobody will be able to predict his own actions, thoughts, theories, poems, etc. before deciding upon them or inventing them. (This is ... a trivial consequence of what it means to 'decide' or 'invent'). So no hope (or danger) exists that cognition of oneself as *en-soi* will cause one to cease to exist *pour-soi*.

3 The complete set of laws which enable these predictions to be made, plus complete descriptions (in atoms-and-the-void terms) of all human beings, would not yet be the whole 'objective truth' about human beings. There would remain as many other distinct sets of such objective truths ... as there were incommensurable vocabularies ... (all those vocabularies within which we attribute beliefs and desires, virtues and beauty).

4 Incommensurability entails irreducibility but not incompatibility, so the failure to 'reduce' these vocabularies to that of 'bottom-level' atoms-and-the-void science casts no doubt upon their cognitive status.

5 The assemblage, *per impossibile*, of all these objective truths
   would still not necessarily be edifying. It might be a picture of a world without a sense, without a moral ...
   Whether his knowledge of the world leaves him with a
   sense of what to do in or with the world is itself predictable, but whether it *should* is not.
6 The fear of science ... of self-objectivation, of being
   turned by too much knowledge into a thing rather than a
   person, is the fear that all discourse will become normal
   discourse ...
7 But the dangers to normal discourse do not come from
   science or naturalistic philosophy. They come from the
   scarcity of food and from the secret police ... (PMN, pp.
   387–9).

Now for some comments:

1 There is a crucial equivocation within (1). Is Rorty claiming that every speech, etc. will turn out to be predictable
under meaningful or hermeneutically adequate descriptions (i)
or not (ii)? If the former, that is to say if every speech, etc. is
completely predictable under hermeneutically adequate descriptions, then (1) is in flagrant contradiction with (3). For (1)
now says in effect that the whole objective truth about human
beings is completely predictable from physical theory. Moreover (1) seems in contradiction with (6). How can there now
be room for abnormal discourse – for 'something new under the
sun, [for] human life as poetic rather than merely contemplative' (PMN, p. 389) – or for (7) 'free and leisured conversation
[generating] abnormal discourse as the sparks fly upward'
(PMN, p. 389). Gone too would be the conditions for the
applicability of the term 'invention' (2) or of the language-game
of moral discourse (5). It seems more likely then that Rorty is
committed only to the latter (ii), viz. the predictability only of
the sounds or movements in which every speech, etc. physically consists. But this horn of the dilemma is equally disastrous for Rorty. For in what sense do uninterpreted sounds
and movements constitute speeches, thoughts, theories,

poems, etc.? Bell's Theorem or Goldbach's Conjecture have to
be intended, uttered and understood for them to be said to be
successfully stated in speech acts. Mere utterance of the
sounds which would constitute them, if interpreted, is not
sufficient. And how can we imagine that these sounds and
movements are predictable before the cultural developments,
contexts and agents have brought them into being – in effect,
before they are determined *qua* caused. This is not to resusci-
tate ghosts, merely to insist on embodied human agency. Nor
does it involve a 'mind-stuff', merely the agentive agency of
creatures who are material beings with emergent powers such
that they are capable of reacting back on the materials out of
which and the levels at which they were originally formed (cf.
PON 1, pp. 124–5; PON 2, pp. 97–8) – as we do in every
action.

2 An atoms-and-the-void theory capable of satisfying the
criteria listed in (1) would be complete and no longer transformable. Rorty's half-truth, viz. his insistence on the transformability of knowledge (in the transitive dimension) (but not the
transfactuality of objects (in the intransitive dimension)), dis-
appears. Such a language would indeed be 'nature's own' (cf.
CIS, chapter 1). Its descriptions would no longer be 'optional'
(cf. PMN, p. 378): they would be basic, foundational and true.
Thus would the dreams of traditional, uncritical realism – on
Rorty's own account of it – be satisfied. Nor is such a theory –
the absolutist pole of his epistemological disjunct (see p. 28
above) – a mere logical posit for Rorty: 'Every speech,
thought, theory, poem, composition and philosophy *will turn
out* to be completely predictable in purely naturalistic terms'
(p. 387, my emphasis). One commentator has even referred in
this context to Rorty's 'deep-seated realism'.[4] And Rorty himself has said: 'Being a materialist is simply putting a bet on
what the vocabulary of the predictive disciplines will turn out
to be.'[5]

3 (5) reaffirms the traditional dichotomy between factual
and evaluative discourse. But to criticize a belief informing an
action is implicitly to criticize the action itself, and if the origin
or source of the belief is found – by explanatory critical sciences

– to lie in some changeable social circumstance a move to a negative evaluation of that circumstance and to a positive evaluation of action rationally directed at transforming it is *ceteris paribus* mandatory, as we shall see in Appendix 1.

4   Martin Hollis has referred to Rorty's 'unrelentingly passive image of persons' (AM, p. 253). Rorty's physicalism and behaviourism does not mesh well with his existentialism and enthusiasm for creative discourse and conversation here. But what unites the two Rortys is their common rejection of the idea of 'mental structure' (cf. Jacek Holówka, in AM, p. 197); and with this goes the idea of a range of crucial emergent powers: all those powers involved in our deliberative executive agency, which is the stuff of our social life. Underlying the rejection of the concept of 'mental structure' is an assumption shared in common by Rorty, Descartes and twentieth-century materialists: namely that the nature of the physical world is such that it excludes the properties associated with 'mind' (cf. Jennifer Hornsby, in AM, chapter 3). The answer to this is not to define the natural world in such a way that the mental cannot be a (synchronically) irreducible part of it (cf. PON, chapter 3.4–5).

Man is always free to choose new descriptions (for, among other things, himself).

PMN, p. 362n

The pivotal opposition between a phenomenal or empirical realm subject to strictly deterministic laws known (or knowable) to science and an intelligible realm of human being (or intentionalistic redescription) where agents are free is a familiar one. The Manichean world of late nineteenth-century German culture fused this broadly Kantian cleavage with Hegelian dichotomies to furnish distinctions between *Erklären* (causal explanation) and *Verstehen* (interpretive understanding), the nomothetic and the ideographic, the repeatable and the unique, the domains of nature and of history. Since then, the pivotal contrast has usually been accompanied by the claim that, in the case of the intelligible order and its denizens, science must at least be complemented (the neo-Kantian position) and at the most be replaced (the dualist anti-naturalist position) by another practice, method or approach – namely, 'hermeneutics'. The grounds for hermeneutics lie in the uniquely meaningful, linguistic or conceptual character of its subject-matter, in virtue of which it is precisely intelligible. So it is with Rorty too. But before we can see this, there is some unravelling to do.

The underlying distinction for Rorty is, as we have seen,

A the Kantian so-called 'existentialist' distinction between people as empirical selves and as moral agents (PMN, p. 382).

It is this, or something very like this, distinction that underpins his critique of epistemology as based on a confusion of 'explanation' and 'justification' (PMN, chapters 3–4) and his praise for Sellars (e.g. at PMN, p. 180n) for insisting on the irreducibility of norms, values and practices to facts and descriptions. (This is compatible with his critique of value-free discourse (PMN, p. 364). For Rorty wants to stress the irreducible normativity of the social and defactualize the social so achieved. (Hence there are no objective (factual) constraints in social reality.)) (A) is grounded, or so I shall argue, in the consideration that it is discourse that is distinctive of human beings: 'people *discourse* whereas things do not' (PMN, p. 347). Without discourse, no statement (or description) could be true or false. Also, without discourse, there would be no abnormal discourse; hence no hermeneutics and no edification; no choice and therefore no *pour-soi*. It is in this sense, I have suggested, that we could sum up his reconciliation of the poles constituting the pervasive tension of PMN by saying that we are determined as material bodies but free as speaking and writing (discursive) subjects. In chapter 8 (A) explicitly comes to the fore as the irreducibility of the *pour-soi* to the *en-soi*.

But before we get to chapter 8, Kant's 'existentialist' distinction (which structures PMN as a whole) has already become displaced or transposed in chapter 7 onto:

B   the 'linguistified'[6] and Kuhnian distinction between normal and abnormal discourse.

Later, by the time of NL (and CIS, chapters 1–3), this distinction has made way for, or passed over into:

C   the romantic distinction between what might be called 'alter-determination' and 'self-creation' (CS, p. 12).

But there are already clear premonitions of this in PMN, e.g. in the attempt to distance the romantic notion of man as self-creative from Cartesian dualism and Kantian constitution (PMN, pp. 346, 358; cf. also CP, pp. 179–81). Alter-determination consists in being made rather than making oneself, and leads to stasis or replication; whereas self-creation consists in self-transformation or self-overcoming. So (C) leads readily to:

D   the Nietzschean distinction between the will to truth and the will to self-overcoming (CL, p. 5; CS, p. 12).

(C) is also the distinction between romanticism and moralism (CC, p. 14) and (D) that between philosophy and poetry.

By now the whole ontological backcloth has shifted. The comprehensive actualism of the naturalistic Rorty has given way to a celebration of contingency. (This is really only the other side of the Humean coin – they are linked in symbiotic interdependency.) Already prefigured in PMN, chapter 8 (p. 381n), this familiar existentialist motif is elaborated into an ontology of the particular, idiosyncratic, accidental and unique. Thus the individuation of human beings – idiographic

particulars – is to be achieved by their capturing their uniqueness in a unique, and so novel, way. Only thus can we avoid
the fate of being the product of some pre-existing set of programmes or formulae, and so merely a copy, replica or instance
of a type (or universal) rather than an *individual*. (It might be
argued that the concept of contingency only makes sense in
relation to that of necessity, which is officially (for Quinean
reasons) disallowed. But Rorty can say his use of it is
a deliberate polemical reactive one, designed to make an (anti-)
philosophical point.)

(B), (C) and (D) constitute the linguistic, romantic and Nietzschean displacements of Rorty's original (in PMN) Kantian
problematic. I am going to argue that discourse is the central
unifying category in Rorty's later thought; and that it determines the progression from (A) through to (D).

In so far as it is discourse that is distinctive of human beings,
we have the possibility of creating new languages (vocabularies, descriptions, etc.), of unfamiliar uses of existing
noises and marks (metaphors) (CL, p. 6), of abnormal and
incommensurable, including reactive and potentially edifying
(including non-constructive) discourses – and hence of *hermeneutics*. Hermeneutics is the generic term for the activity of
rendering intelligible what is at present unintelligible (PMN,
p. 321). It is the attempt to normalize discourse – that is,
paradigmatically it is discourse (from within some normal
discourse) about abnormal rather than normal discourse
(PMN, p. 346). Hermeneutics is a kind of meta-discourse; but
one that is only needed in the case of some incommensurable,
and therefore (from the standpoint of the hermeneutical en-
quirer) abnormal, discourse. It is the attempt to forge a 'common context of utterance' or 'mutual horizon' (PON 1, pp.
197ff; PON 2, pp. 154ff). Note that 'there is no requirement
that people should be more difficult to understand than
things; it is merely that people discourse whereas things do
not. What makes the difference is not discourse versus silence
but incommensurable discourses versus commensurable discourses' (PMN, p. 347).

In Part 3 of PMN, hermeneutics is somewhat oddly counterposed to epistemology, which is thereby severed from its specific connections to science, scepticism, the theory of knowledge and philosophy. What they share in common is that they are both meta-discourses, discourses not about the world, but about our knowledge (epistemology) or discourse (hermeneutics) about the world. What differentiates them is that epistemology presupposes universal commensuration, underpinned by the figure of what I have called the 'ontic fallacy' (see p. 32 above); whereas hermeneutics does not, and in fact is necessary just when this assumption breaks down – when we must 'savour' or 'bandy about', in order to literalize or normalize a new or different way of speaking (cf. CL, p. 6). A directly connected peculiarity is Rorty's restriction of hermeneutics to discourse about abnormal (or incommensurable normal) rather than normal discourse. This is explained by Rorty's 'hypernormalization' of normal discourse (noted on p. 29 above). By contrast, I would argue that hermeneutics, or the interpretative understanding of meaningful objects, is *always* necessary in social life – and *within* it, as well as about it. (Thus there is hermeneutics in normal physics or chemistry.)

On the interpretation of Rorty I am developing, the fundamental feature of human beings, their discursivity, gives us their ontological duality: as both 'generators of new descriptions' and 'beings one hopes to be able to describe accurately', 'as both *pour-soi* and *en-soi*, as both described objects and describing subjects' (PMN, p. 378). As describing subjects, human beings can redescribe every object, in new, including potentially abnormal (and hence incommensurable normal) ways – which is to say that because human beings are (re)describing subjects, new, and potentially incommensurable, descriptions can become true of *any* object.

But Rorty does not clearly or explicitly distinguish the case (a) where any object (including human beings) may *change*, and so require a new, potentially incommensurable, description from the case (b) where any object (including human beings) may, though *unchanged*, be redescribed in a new, potentially incommensurable, way. To make this distinction explicitly requires disambiguating intransitive from transitive change. Thus it is characteristic of Rorty that, having allowed that 'for all we know, it may be that human creativity has dried up, and that in the future it will be the *non*human which squirms out of our conceptual net' (PMN, p. 351), he goes on to add that in such a case 'it is natural to start talking about an unknown language – to imagine, for example, the migrating butterflies having a language in which they describe features of the world for which Newtonian mechanics has no name' (PMN, p. 352).

For Rorty, then:

1 All things may be redescribed, even if they do not change, possibly in terms of an incommensurable vocabulary.
2 All things may exhibit novelty, and so require a new, potentially incommensurable discourse.
3 Only human beings can discourse (normally or abnormally, literally or metaphorically). And:
4 Only human beings can overcome themselves, their past and their fellow human beings – and they do so in and by (creating a new) discourse in terms of a new incommensurable vocabulary.

It should be stressed that for Rorty everything is susceptible to a new, potentially incommensurable, description. He says that: 'It would have been fortunate had Sartre followed up his remark that man is the being whose essence is to have no essence by saying that this went for all other beings also' (PMN, pp. 361–2, n. 7). And he adds that the point is that 'man is always free to choose new descriptions (for, among other things, himself)'. But of course, the addendum is not true of beings other than man. Snakes and stones, migrating butterflies and runner beans are not free to choose new descriptions. Of course, some kinds of things (e.g. carbon atoms, dogs) but not others (e.g. tables, chairs) have essences (cf. RTS, p. 210). But can Rorty be interpreted as meaning anything other than (a) that discourse is the essence of man[7] and/or (b) that in so far as man has no specific essence (no 'species being'), he is the being whose essence, *qua* describing and redescribing subject, is to be the essence or measure of all beings, *qua* describable and redescribable objects.[8] Discourse, then, is the essence of man; and, through man, of being. This, if my interpretation is correct, is the residue of Rorty's 'linguistic turn'. It chimes in well with Gadamer's dictum that 'being is manifest in language', which itself reflects Heidegger's proposition that 'language is the house of being'.[9]

What is the connection between (A) and (B)? There is a contingent overlap between them in the sense that the science/non-science distinction gives way to the normal/abnormal distinction, and, as it so happens, the redescribable world of human beings (culture) is caught less well than the redescribable world of nature by the normal (scientific) discourse of the day (for any or all of reasons 1–4). Thus there is no historiographically relevant demarcation criterion, 'no deeper difference than that between what happens in "normal" and in "abnormal" discourse' – a 'distinction which cuts across [and effectively replaces] the distinction between science and nonscience' (PMN, p. 333). And 'that portion of the field of enquiry where we feel rather uncertain that we have the right vocabulary at hand and that portion where we feel rather certain that we do ... does, at the moment, roughly coincide with the distinction between the fields of the *Geistes*- and the *Naturwissenschaften*' (PMN, p. 352).

What then becomes of freedom? It ceases to be understood merely negatively, as grounded in our ignorance of physicalistically determining laws, and becomes, through our capacity to *redescribe* that world (or relevant bits of it), something which is both positive and humanistically more recognizable – namely, the capacity to create, and choose between, different vocabularies – that is, to write or speak (and in CP also to read (and presumably to hear)) *abnormally*. (Thus: 'Sartre tells us we are not going to have ... a way of seeing freedom as nature (or, less cryptically, a way of seeing our creation of, and choice between, vocabularies in the same "normal" way as we see ourselves *within* one of those vocabularies)' (PMN, p. 380).) Freedom, then, is shown in the exercise of our capacity for abnormal discourse – for instance, in fantasy and

metaphor. Such discourse is, of course, always parasitic on
the weighty existence of normal, literal, public, 'stodgy' discourse (CC, p. 14). Moreover, it presupposes a degree of
leisure and the absence of debilitating toil or pain (CS, p. 14).

Freedom as the capacity to engage in abnormal discourse is
closely linked to 'freedom as the recognition of contingency'
(CS, p. 11). Recognition here consists in the use or appropria-
tion of particular contingencies – which amounts to 'redescribing them' (CS, p. 14). However, it appears to be only the
human world, where things are meaningful in character,
which can be redescribed in this way. This is particularly clear
in the case of our dealings with fellow human beings. 'In
coping with other persons ... we can overcome contingency
and pain ... by appropriating and transforming their language.' But in relation to the 'non-human, the non-linguistic,
we no longer have the ability to overcome contingency and
pain, but only to recognise [it]' (CS, p. 14). This is, as it were,
a Davidsonian variant of the Vichian *facimus*. We can know
the social world not so much in so far as we have made it, but
in so far as we have remade or reappropriated it by redescribing it in our own terms. 'The final victory of poetry in its
ancient quarrel with philosophy – the final victory of
metaphors of self-creation over metaphors of discovery –
would consist in our becoming reconciled to the thought that
this is the only sort of power over the world which we can
hope to have.[10] For that would be the final abjuration of the
notion that truth, and not just power and pain, is to be found
"out there"' (CS, p. 14; CIS, p. 40).

We have got slightly ahead of ourselves. So let us retrace
our steps. Though determined as material bodies, which includes the movements of our larynxes and writing hands, we
are free as writing and speaking (discursive) subjects – a
freedom shown most signally in the exercise of our capacity
for abnormal discourse. A criterion of political value flows
directly from this, namely:

B'   'It is central to the idea of a liberal society that, in
     respect of words as opposed to deeds, persuasion as

opposed to force, anything goes' (CC, p. 11; CIS, pp. 51–2).

Later, as we shall see, this formula gets modified.

What is this Rorty's supreme value? It is (C) romantic self-creation, which becomes, by the time of NL, (D) Nietzschean self-overcoming. Man is the describing, redescribing being. Among the entities man can redescribe in a new, and abnormal way, is himself. By making a new, incommensurable, description of herself 'stick', she makes it true; and thus 'gives birth to' (to use Harold Bloom's term) or 'creates' herself – which is to say 'overcomes' her previous or past self. Moreover, only by describing herself in a totally novel way can she capture and express her idiosyncrasy or uniqueness – or rather achieve it, i.e. achieve her individuation – for anything less would reduce her to a (more or less complex set of) formula(e), a token of a type (or set of types). Such radical self-description (which could be nicknamed 'me-' or 'we-' description) is the highest form of description. For not only does the redescription redescribe the redescriber, but in the process of redescription – of winning it, of making it stick, of achieving recognition for it – the (re)description is made true; so achieving the identity of subject and object, by *creating* it. This, *if* it were possible would be the historic goal of philosophy achieved in a romantic or Nietzschean mode.[11]

Man, then, by redescribing himself, a redescribing subject, in a totally new way and winning acceptance for it, creates a new identity or subjectivity for herself – and thus (potentially) for every other object in the universe too, which can be redescribed in accordance with the new image, in her own way. (For she is the genus of all genera, the *anima mundi* through which language speaks.) Self-creation by self-overcoming is the reconciliation of man as empirical subject and as moral agent, as described object and describing subject, the realization of the reconciliation between nature and spirit which Kant vainly tried to achieve in *The Critique of Judgement* by recourse to a divinizing as-if, now accomplished in the process of discursive self-formation. Freed from the shackles of nature by her poetic power or discursive agency, by creating new descriptions of herself or her tradition which stick, or 'take' in the community (perhaps after her death), and so become true, she overcomes, i.e. remakes, herself or her tradition. Such overcoming redescriptions are redescriptions of redescriptions of a (fully determined) physical world; and there is no criterion for their truth other than their acceptance. 'The Nietzschean substitution of self-creation for discovery substitutes a picture of the hungry generations treading each other down for a picture of humanity approaching closer to the light' (CL, p. 6; CIS, p. 20). On this moving staircase of history, stories replace stories, and there is nothing more to this process than the prosaic quasi-Darwinian fact that some stories which are told stick around for a while (are retold), while most do not.

Is the romantic/Nietzschean ideal – of total self-creation, complete self-overcoming – possible? Clearly not. Nor does Rorty think it is attainable. On the contrary, the new way of speaking can only be (a) marginal or partial; (b) recognized *post festum* and retrospectively justified; and (c) conditional on future acceptance or usage. (a) A total transformation would leave the discursive agent and her community without the linguistic resources to recognize or refer to her achievement; nor could it be literalized in the community unless there were some continuity or overlap in usage. 'Overcoming' is always piecemeal and partial – transformation, not replacement; and it respects the existential intransitivity of the self or past to be overcome. (b) Clearly the self-overcoming discourse must be abnormal. But if it is abnormal, how can it come to be understood, i.e. normalized? Rorty's answer is that: 'If it is savoured rather than spat out, the sentence may be repeated, caught up, bandied about. Then it will gradually require a habitual use, a familiar place in the language-game' (CL, p. 6; CIS, p. 18). I would prefer to consider the way in which something akin to a logic of analogy, metaphor and new meaning or use is implicit in our scientific, literary, artistic, political (etc.) judgements and practices. This would also be a logic of determinate negation and immanent critique. (c) Because the self-overcoming process must be public[12] (for Hegelian as well as Wittgensteinian reasons), 'there can be no fully Nietzschean lives ... no lives that are not largely parasitical upon an un-redescribed past and dependent on the charity of yet un-born generations' (CS, p. 15; CIS, p. 42).

Despite the way Rorty refrains from finding an identical subject-object here, and so distances himself from romantic and Nietzschean ideals, his account of the social world is one in which romantic and Nietzschean processes are the vital ones, with the paradigmatic human being (= *Übermensch*) being the strong poet (or utopian revolutionary) who manages to impose her vision, even if only marginally, retrospectively and conditionally, upon a tradition or a community. (In the former case, she becomes a member of a discontinuous series, whose fate it is to be continually reappropriated in a Whig-gishly continuous narrative. In the latter case, she becomes a self whose self-description 'counts' and is acknowledged in the stories which are told and repeated.) In any event Rorty has already subscribed to one identical subject–object – that implicit in the Humean–Kantian story of a world known by (at least natural) science,[13] which remains empirical, actual and contingent – rather than real, transfactually efficacious and characterized by natural necessity (cf. RTS, chapter 3.3, 3.5 and 3.6). And it is this world which, I argued above, makes discursive, as much as any other socialized, open-systemic form of human agency, impossible. For such agency depends upon the agent 'making a difference' to the material world.

(A) to (D) between them let us score four progressively richer degrees of freedom in Rorty.

$Freedom_0$ – as susceptibility to new descriptions, discourses. This is freedom as caprice. It depends upon the sense in which, through man, discourse speaks being – the sense in which man is *anima mundi*.
$Freedom_1$ – as the capacity to give new descriptions, generate new discourses. This is a sense in which freedom is connected with being a moral agent, *pour-soi* and capable of justification and radical choice.

Freedom$_2$ – as the capacity to engage in metaphor, fantasy and abnormal discourse (revolutionary practice?). This is freedom as abnormal discourse – in which it is said, for instance, that the dangers to 'abnormal discourse do not come from science or naturalistic philosophy – they come from the scarcity of food and the secret police' (PMN, p. 389). This is linked to freedom as the recognition of contingency – the contingencies that we seize on and appropriate in poetry and fantasy. Politically, it licenses the slogan that 'in words, as opposed to deeds ... anything goes' (CC, p. 11; CIS p. 52). Its text is Mill's *On Liberty*.

Freedom$_3$ – as the capacity to generate radically new self-descriptions, and to break free from or overcome the past. This is the highest degree of freedom. It remains an individual project. Freudian or Nietzschean moral psychology cannot be used to define social goals; nor is there any bridge between a private ethic of self-becoming and a public ethic of mutual accommodation (CS, p. 12; CIS, p. 34).

Freedom, then, as caprice, discourse, capricious discourse and creative discourse. I turn now to the question, 'How is freedom possible?'

NOTES

1 See P. Manicas, *A History and Philosophy of the Social Sciences*, Oxford, 1987, p. 307.
2 P. Winch, *The Idea of a Social Science*, London, 1958, p. 115. Cf. also PMN, p. 348.
3 Cf. M. Hollis, in AM, p. 247.
4 J. Holówka, in AM, p. 190.
5 Interview, *Radical Philosophy 32* (1982), p. 4.
6 This expression is taken from R. Rorty, 'Posties', *London Review of Books*, 3 September 1987, p. 12. It signifies here roughly the transition from epistemology to linguistic philosophy – the 'linguistic turn' (the title of an important collection of essays and documents Rorty edited (Chicago, 1967) (henceforth LT)). What I have been calling the 'epistemic fallacy' (see p. 8 above) is now

expressed in a linguistic form as the definition of being in terms of our discourse about being (cf. PON 1, pp. 171, 198–9; PON 2, pp. 133, 155–6).

7 In this context it is worth bearing in mind Rorty's rejection of the concept of human nature. 'Humanity' does not have 'a nature over and above the various forms of human life which history has thrown up so far' (CC, p. 13). It would surely be wiser for Rorty to argue not that there is no such thing as human nature, but rather that (i) it always manifests itself in some historically specific and socially mediated form, and (ii) it is and must always be known under some historically particular – and therefore potentially transformable – description.

8 Note the similarity with the Renaissance theme of man as the being that is the 'genus of all empirical genera', '*creatura commune*', or '*anima mundi*'. See L. Colletti, *Marxism and Hegel*, London, 1973, chapter 11.

9 'Letter on humanism', *Philosophy in the 20th Century*, ed. W. Barrett and H. Aiken. New York, 1961.

10 Rorty seems in his rhetoric to have forgotten entirely about technology, which involves the transfactual application of (discovered) laws.

11 There is some irony in the fact that the successful strong poet or utopian revolutionary would realize the goal of, of all discourses, philosophy.

12 Though Rorty does sometimes imply the contrary: 'Any seemingly random constellation of . . . things can set the tone of a life. Any such constellation can set up an unconditional commitment to whose service a life may be devoted – a commandment no less unconditional because it may be intelligible to, at best, only one person' (CS, p. 12).

13 Even if the epistemic fallacy is now committed in a linguistically transposed mode.

4

How is Freedom Possible?

What sort of freedom is at issue here? Freedom, for example, 'from the scarcity of food and the secret police' (PMN, p. 389). Or from being so 'racked by pain' or 'immersed in toil' (CS, p. 14) as to be unable to engage in abnormal discourse; or from being too uneducated to be capable of edification (PMN, pp. 365–6); or from being too unleisured – to lack the time or the equipment – to create metaphors (CS, p. 14), fantasies or poetry or generate a new description of oneself, one's culture or one's past. This kind of freedom – freedom$_1$–freedom$_3$ – depends, I am going to argue, upon the explanatory-emancipatory critical human sciences. Such sciences do not yet exist – but they are struggling to burst into being. We stand to them today in the same kind of position as Descartes and Hobbes stood to the infant giant of mechanics (PMN, p. 131). And the present book seeks to 'underlabour' for these new sciences in the way, a little later, Locke sought to under-labour for mechanics (cf. CC, p. 11).

How then is such freedom possible? Very briefly and schematically:

1 The *sui generis* reality and causal efficacy of social forms, on a strictly physical criterion, in terms of their making a difference to the state of the material world which would otherwise have occurred (from soil erosion and acid rain

through to the production of some rather than other noises and marks), has to be recognized (see PON 1, p. 50; PON 2, p. 39).

2 The existence of objective social structures (from languages to family or kinship systems to economic or state forms) dependent on the reproductive and transformative agency of human beings, must be granted. Such structures are not created by human beings – for they pre-exist us and their existence is a necessary condition for any intentional act. But they exist and persist only in virtue of our activity, which reproduces or transforms them. In our everyday practices of substantive *poiesis* or making, which consists in or involves the transformation, in various media, of what is to hand – (paper, a musical score, raw meat, steel) – we reproduce or transform the social world itself. In general, changes in social structures will reflect or be reflected in changes in the transformative agency which would otherwise reproduce them.

These social structures are concept-dependent, but not merely conceptual. Thus a person could not be said to be 'unemployed' or 'out of work' unless she and the other relevant agents possessed some (not necessarily correct or fully adequate) concept of that condition and were able to give some sort of account of it, namely to describe (or redescribe) it. But it *also* involves, for instance, her being physically excluded from certain sites, definite locations in space and time. That is to say, social life always has a material dimension (and leaves some physical trace) (see PON 1, p. 174; PON 2, p. 136).

3 It follows from this that Rorty's distinction between 'coping with other persons' and 'coping with the non-human, the non-linguistic' namely by redescription and recognition respectively (noted on p. 64 above) needs to be reworked – on several counts. First, there is more to coping with social reality than coping with other people. There is coping with a whole host of social entities, including institutions, traditions, networks of relations and the like – which are irreducible to people.[1] In particular, it would be a mistake to think that we had overcome a social structure, like the economy, state or

family, if we were successful in imposing our description of it on the community. This holds in the case of people (including ourselves) too – we need to explain and sometimes change them (ourselves) as well as to (re)describe them adequately (productively, fruitfully, and so on). Think once more of the Rortian ideal – the strong poet (or utopian revolutionary) who can redescribe the already determined world in accordance with their vision – who can, retrospectively, by making their descriptions of themselves or their society true (by winning acceptance for them), (re)make themselves or their society. If there are objective social and psychic (as well as natural) structures – structures that need to be tackled before or so that we can become free (even in order to do poetry) – such a victory may prove a Pyrrhic one.

This point may also be put by saying that there is more to normative social science than creative redescription. Rorty says: 'To see a common social practice as cruel and unjust . . . is a matter of redescription rather than discovery. It is a matter of changing vocabularies rather than of stripping away the veil of appearances from an objective reality, an experimentation with new ways of speaking rather than of overcoming "false consciousness"' (CC, p. 14). But the identification of the *source* of an experienced injustice in social reality, necessary for changing or remedying it, involves much more than redescription, even if it depends on that too centrally. It is a matter of finding and disentangling webs of relations in social life, and engaging explanatory critiques of the practices that sustain them. This may indeed often involve the detection of various types of false and otherwise unhappy consciousness (and more generally being). And this in turn may lead on to *critiques* of the vocabularies and conceptual systems in which they are expressed, and the additional social practices with which they are implicated. Moreover, such explanatory critiques will lead, *ceteris paribus*, to action rationally directed to transforming, dissolving or disconnecting the structures and relations which explain the experience of injustice and the other ills theoretically informed practice has diagnosed. Poets, like philosophers, need to think of explaining to change, rather than just reinterpreting or redescribing to edify, the world.

On the other hand, there is more to coping with nature than mere recognition – or that plus redescription. For a start, as I have already suggested, we need hermeneutics in everyday natural science and not just to render intelligible abnormal theoretical redescriptions of nature. Secondly, it should be stressed that just as our conscious interventions in nature, for instance, in natural science and technology, are symbolically mediated, so we intervene in nature in all our causal interactions with the world, including our dialogues with the fellow members of our kind. The social world is not a cut-off redescription of nature. Rather, it is both inscribed within and in continuous dynamic causal interaction with (the rest of) nature. To fail to see this, and in particular that there are physical (natural) constraints on human social life – namely 'non-human forces to which we must be responsible' (CC, p. 10) and responsive – is a charter for ecological disaster, if not indeed (species) suicide.

The social and the socially conditioned or affected parts of the natural world are potentially transformable by human beings. But there may be some absolutes (universals, constants) of significance for human beings – which they just have to accept or 'recognize'. For example, fundamental laws of nature, the scarcity of some natural resources, upper limits to ecologically sustainable economic growth, aspects of human nature, the fact of the finitude (if not the precise duration) of human existence. The existence of *absolute* must not be confused with the existence of *objective* structures. Social structures may be just as objective, and transfactually efficacious within their geo-historical domain, as natural laws. Moreover, both alike typically impose limits and constraints upon the kinds of action (including speech action) possible to human beings, without (normally) rigidly determining what we do within those limits or constraints (see RTS, chapter 2.5).

The other side of the supposition that our movements are determined is the notion that our talk, discourse, is free. What does it mean, in this context, to hold that 'man is always free to choose new descriptions (for, among other things, himself)' (PMN, p. 362n)? I have argued in chapter 2 against Rorty that we are not compelled or determined in our beliefs or descriptions (any more than we are in most of our other states or actions – all of which depend on or manifest themselves in or through the movements of our bodies). But it does not follow from this that nature or society does not impose *constraints* on our rationally justifiable talk. Suppose this doctrine is coupled with the collapse of the intransitive dimension, in which current theory takes the place of the ontological realm (a realm that, I have argued (on p. 26 above), we need, philosophically, precisely to think the objective existence and efficacy of structures independently of our current theory of them). It is now easy to see how the notion that 'man is always free to choose new descriptions' can encourage the voluntaristic position that man is always free to choose *any* description – or at any rate, any description that society, in the form of his peers (in the transitive dimension), will let him get away with – which is more or less the Rortian doctrine here (see PMN, pp. 176ff).[2]

Such voluntarism may not do much damage in the normal discourse of the natural sciences, but in the abnormal discourses of the social sciences and the other humanities which are already in crisis and do appeal not just to irrelevant but to absurd and patently inapplicable philosophies (like positivism (see PON, chapter 4.2; SR, chapter 3.7)), it may encourage a superficial theoretical Maoism, which masks or screens the absence of real intellectual progress (or social change – where it may be a case of *plus ça change, plus c'est la même chose*). The successful poet's life may now become an incessant succession of fleeting paradigm shifts in which even aesthetic enhancement begins to pale.

Of course these (intransitive) objective structures at work in nature and society, whether transhistorical or not, must always be described in a (transitive) more or less historically transient language, i.e. in terms of potentially transformable descriptions.[3] (But there will be objective constraints on rational linguistic change too – constraints other than those imposed by sheer poetic power, although the latter will, in context, be among them.)

4 In virtue of the fact that efficacious reasons are causes of intentional behaviour, not just redescriptions of them, the agent's account of her reasons has a special authority, which a neo-Kantian dualism cannot ground (see PON, chapter 3.2; SR, chapter 2.4) – but this authority is not absolute. Rather, it is subject to negotiation, as we come to understand better, both in general and in the individual case, 'how we work' (*contra* PMN, p. 258), that is, what makes us do the apparently irrational or otherwise explanatorily interesting things we do. (One consequence of this is that language can change us, as in 'the talking cure', but also when inspired by poetry (*contra* PMN, p. 185).) Unconscious motivation and tacit skills are only two of the sources of opacity in social life; others are acknowledged conditions and unintended consequences (SR, chapter 2.2). So although society is a skilled accomplishment of agents, it does not follow from this that theoretical social science (informed by participants' understanding) is redundant. The task of the theoretical social sciences will be to establish the structural conditions, consequences and contours of the phenomenologically experienced world. In some, perhaps many, cases the critical redescription and structural explanation of that experience, and the accounts given or based on it, will be necessary.

5 In so far as an agent is interested in preserving or extending or deepening or gaining some freedom, this will always involve trying to understand, in the sense of explaining, the character of some social or socially conditioned or affectable entity, structure or thing – in order to maintain (reproduce) or change (transform) or otherwise dissolve or defuse, or to stimulate or release it. To become or remain 'free', in the simple sense of being 'unconstrained', always *potentially* involves both a theory of those constraints and, in so far as the freedom is feasible, a practice of liberation or liberty preservation. One may be free or desire freedom, in this sense, from any kind of thing.

On the other hand, emancipation, and more especially self-emancipation, involves:

1 A stronger sense of being 'free', namely as knowing, possessing the power and the disposition to act in or towards one's real interests (cf. SR, p. 170). And:
2 A stronger sense of 'liberation', namely as consisting in the transformation of unneeded, unwanted and oppressive to needed, wanted and empowering *sources* of determination.

Emancipation, that is to say, depends upon the transformation of structures rather than just the amelioration of states of affairs. And it will, at least in the case of self-emancipation, depend in particular upon a conscious transformation in the transformative activity or praxis of the social agents concerned. As such, emancipation is *necessarily* informed by explanatory social theory.

The emancipatory social sciences may, for their part, take as their starting point some human need or aspiration (say for poetry) and enquire into the natural and social conditions (if any) of its non-fulfilment. Or they may begin with an immanent critique of prevailing social theories or ideologies, which may move on to the explanatory critique of falsity-generating (cf. PMN, p. 282) or otherwise malevolent (ill-producing) social structures (see SR, chapter 2.5–2.7). In either case, the social sciences will be participants in a theory – practice dialectic or spiral with the emancipatory practices concerned. In this process the kind of creative radical self or society redescriptions, to which Rorty calls our attention, may play a vital role in individuation or identity (including group and kind (or species) identity) formation. And this activity of *seeing themselves under a new description which they have helped to create*, will generally figure crucially in the *transformed transformative praxis* of the self-emancipating agents.

There is no need to deny either social scientific knowledge or a metatheory of it to make the world safe for poets. For a society (or person) that has no use for poetry will *need* it more than most; and for that it will require that kind of knowledge of its situation which only the emergent human sciences can aspire to provide. Such sciences will always depend on poets; just as poets to be free, among other things to write or speak their lines, may, in the contemporary world, have to have recourse to the explanatory sciences as well as to their redescriptive powers. As for philosophers, if they follow the sounder part of Rorty's advice and give up the search for permanent, neutral, a-historical compulsive foundations of knowledge (which I have called the 'ontic fallacy'), they may find that, by focusing on the historical arts and sciences and the other social practices, as they are, have come down to us and may yet develop, there is more than a little critical underlabouring (including further de-divinizing) to do . . .

NOTES

1 Of course, Rorty would probably acknowledge this – but there is more than a hint of methodological individualism in PMN (see e.g. p. 206).
2 Rorty's argument that the difference between the 'kooky' and the 'revolutionary' (PMN, p. 339) or 'fantasy' and 'genius' (CS, p. 14) is the difference between ways of speaking which, for various contingencies, just happen to 'catch on' with other people or 'take' in the community overlooks the point that, for instance, existential, explanatory and other claims in the intransitive dimension (including successful predictions under repeatable conditions) plus formal proofs, demonstrations of anomaly resolution (among a bundle of historically discernible criteria) have to be satisfied in a revolutionary situation in science before intellectual progress can be definitely said to have occurred. There is reason, albeit often disguised, in intellectual revolutions; and such reason does not impede, but is shown, in part, in its poetry.
3 However, Rorty tends persistently to exaggerate the degree of 'Kuhn-loss', that is to say, the extent to which subjects are changed, problems are set aside or displaced rather than resolved, anomalies are repressed or forgotten instead of being cleared up or normalized, in scientific and more generally discursive change. (In this his practice is at one with his theory.) In consequence he tends to underestimate the extent to which reference is maintained (or agents continue to 'talk about' the same thing) through change.

Part III

Politics

5

Self-defining versus Social Engineering – Poetry and Politics: The Problem-field of *Contingency, Irony and Solidarity*

Redescribing ourselves is the most important thing we do.
PMN, pp. 358–9

If the problem-field of PMN is defined by the tension between (α) our determination as material bodies and (β) our freedom as discursive (speaking, writing, reading, listening) subjects, that of CIS is defined by that between (β) this freedom or our poetic licence, as expressed in private irony and (γ) public pragmatism, as realized in a liberal political culture. Rorty wishes to subscribe to both. But just as in PMN Rorty neglects the material embodiment of human agency in an untenable distinction between the physical and the personal, so in CIS Rorty neglects the social realization of human agency in an untenable distinction between the private and the public.

It is clear that Rorty's romanticism and poeticism – what he will call his ironism in CIS – is at least in *prima facie* conflict with his Dewey-invoking pragmatism and liberalism. For as one commentator has bluntly put it: 'Rorty's picture of this [poetic] culture as one in which new linguistic forms are constantly killing off old ones, seems better suited to a politics of permanent revolution than to liberalism.'[1] Here again Rorty is aware of the tension – for he notes 'redescription often humiliates' (CIS, p. 90). For Rorty two projects are ends-in-themselves: self-invention and the expansion of the present 'we' or moral community (CIS, p. 64n). And the stress between (β') our own private perfection and (γ') the well-being and happiness of others (between in effect Kant's two duties for men) is to be resolved in what Rorty calls his 'ideal world order' or *summum bonum* which he describes as an 'intricately textured collage of private narcissism and public pragmatism'.[2] More specifically, it is to be resolved in CIS by the privatization of irony, thus reserving the public sphere for pragmatic social engineering. The terms of this solution are immediately debatable: into which sphere – the poetic or the public – does *The Satanic Verses* or even more pointedly CIS itself fall? (From which side of the line is the line itself drawn?)

The tension emerges for the first time in CP, chapter 8 – the 1980 essay, '19th-century idealism and 20th-century textualism'. Here Rorty argues that just as metaphysical idealism, treating the world as if it contained nothing but ideas, was the philosophical form of romanticism, its post-philosophical form is 'textualism', which treats the world as if it contained nothing but texts. Note both idealism and textualism effect the transitivization of being, the former epistemologically, the latter in a linguistified key. Textualism is post-philosophical in the sense that it recognizes that philosophy and science are now relatively secondary features of a disciplinary landscape centred on literature and the practice of literary criticism. Pragmatism is the post-philosophical form of philosophy (CP, p. 143). (By CIS the textualist has given way to the ironist, who discharges the burden of the romantic impulse in Rortyism; and the pragmatist has become the liberal.) And the problem is this:

> Put in the pragmatist's own cost-accounting terms, [the moral objection to textualism] says that the stimulus to the intellectual's private moral imagination provided by his strong misread-

ings, by his search for sacred wisdom, is purchased at the price of his separation from his fellow-humans.... I think that this moral objection states the really important issue about textualism and pragmatism. But I have no ready way to dispose of it. I should like to do so by drawing a further distinction among strong textualists – a distinction between, for example, Bloom and Foucault. Bloom is a pragmatist in the manner of James, whereas Foucault is a pragmatist in the manner of Nietzsche. Pragmatism appears in James and Bloom as an identification with the struggles of finite men. In Foucault and Nietzsche it appears as contempt for one's own finitude.... Bloom's way of dealing with texts preserves our sense of a common human finitude by moving back and forth between the poet and his poem. Foucault's way of dealing with texts is designed to eliminate the author – and indeed the very idea of 'man' – altogether. I have no wish to defend Foucault's inhumanism, and every wish to praise Bloom's sense of our common human lot. But I do not know how to back up this preference with argument, or even with a precise account of the relevant differences. To do so would involve a full-scale discussion of the possibility of combining private fulfilment, self-realization, with public morality, a concern for justice. (CP, p. 158)

This is, of course, the project of CIS. But in CIS the distinction between humanistic and anti-humanistic textualists is replaced with the distinction between textualism or ironism *per se*, which is to be private and need not be humane, and our public morality, which is to be liberal and kind.

This tension emerges most sharply synchronically – within the structure of CIS – when Rorty acknowledges that the ironist's activity of redescription can *hurt* people. Adopting Judith Shklar's criterion for a liberal: someone who believes that cruelty is the worst thing we do,[3] the problem comes into focus at CIS, pp. 89–90:

Ironism ... results from awareness of the power of redescription. But most people do not want to be redescribed. They want to be taken on their own terms – taken seriously just as they are and just as they talk. The ironist tells them that the language they speak is up for grabs by her and her kind. There is something potentially very cruel about that claim. For the best way to cause people long-lasting pain is to humiliate them by making the things that seem most important to them look futile, obsolete and powerless. Consider what happens when a child's possessions – the little things around which he weaves fantasies that makes him a little different from all other children – are redescribed as 'trash' and thrown away. Or consider what happens when those possessions are made to look ridiculous alongside the possessions of another, richer, child ... Redescription often humiliates.

To this Rorty has a line of limited defence. He notes that the non-ironist, e.g. realist, intellectual is also concerned to redescribe people and their activities (e.g. in terms of a contingently critical hermeneutics (PON 1, p. 177; PON 2, p. 138)). But the ironist cannot present his redescription as empowering or emancipating by claiming to isolate structures of oppression to be thrown off or underlying natures to be revealed and realized, so that he cannot be 'dynamic' or 'progressive' as a realist can profess to be. 'She cannot claim that adopting her redescription of yourself or your situation makes you better able to conquer the forces which are marshalled against you. On her account, that ability is a matter of weapons and luck, not a matter of having truth on your side, or having detected the "movement of history"' (CIS, p. 91).

This problem – of the potentially humiliating and so illiberal character of ironist activity – is an index of the underlying tension between two thought-strands or impulses in Rorty: a romantic and a pragmatic one. As Nancy Fraser has pointed out in an illuminating article,[4] Rorty oscillates between three different ways of dealing with the tension, which I will call the 'complementarity', 'opposition' and 'separation' positions. (These correspond roughly to what Fraser calls the 'invisible hand', 'sublimity or decency' and 'partition' resolutions.) At times, as in CC, he sees freedom for intellectuals as the best way of ensuring that existing descriptions of practices and institutions which may later come to be seen as cruel and unjust do not calcify. At other times, as in the above passage in CIS, he sees the dark side of romanticism as at odds with social kindness and decency, and the ironist intellectual as necessarily alienated from his society and parasitic upon and reactive to the doings of the non-ironist majority (CIS, chapter 4). Rorty's ideal is the liberal ironist. Although he claims at CIS, p. xv that ironism 'in the relevant sense' can be universal, he argues in the text of the book that ironism is necessarily parasitic and reactive. There is thus a split in Rorty's *summum bonum* not only between the public and the private (and, as we shall see, within the self), but between the intellectual ironist minority and the non-intellectual non-ironist majority.[5] This latter is currently metaphysical, but may become nominalist and historicist, while still non-ironist (cf. CIS, p. 87). Finally, in the official solution of CIS, Rorty comes to see ironism as restricted to the purely private sphere, as having no political implications or obligations, with liberalism thus free and able to flourish in the public domain, without interfering with our own private projects of 'self-invention'. Note that if the official position were tenable, there would be no reason in principle against universal ironism. Discounting the actual division of labour, wealth and time in society, why should the project of self-invention be restricted to only some – a privileged elite? No wonder that Rorty has been hailed as an ideologue of and for 'the chattering classes'.[6]

Let us now examine the terms of Rorty's problem and solution(s) in more detail. Rorty's objective is to reconcile romanticism, emblematized in the narcissism of the self-fashioning or strong poet (in the sense explicated in chapter 3) – (β) – with pragmatism, emblematized in the civic-mindedness of the problem-solving reformer – (γ) – eventually in the figure of the liberal ironist, whose ironism is private and liberalism public.

1 On the complementarity or invisible hand position, romanticism and pragmatism are 'natural partners'. Fraser provides a concise summary of this position (already criticized at p. 72 above): 'Only by making society safe for poets can we ensure that language keeps changing. And only by ensuring that language keeps changing can we prevent the normalization of current practices, which might later look cruel and

unjust. Thus, to make society safe for poets is to help make it safe for everyone' (AM, p. 307). So it is not really elitist to 'treat democratic societies as existing for the sake of intellectuals' (CC, p. 14). Moreover, a society organized around poetry and play (whose source lies in anxiety and whose mode is comic), rather than philosophy and science (whose source lies in wonder and whose mode is tragic) would harbour decency and kindness. It would counteract our liability to a specifically human form of suffering, viz. the humiliation that results from being redescribed in another's terms while one's own self-description is peremptorily dismissed. The best safeguard against this sort of cruelty is awareness of other people's vocabularies, best acquired by reading lots of books. The ideal 'aestheticized culture', fostering a cosmopolitan literary intelligentsia, would take as its hero the 'strong poet' who spins off imaginative redescriptions of our predicament, rather than the scientist who seeks to ground our practices in facts. Such a culture 'has no ideal except freedom, no goal except a willingness to see how [free and open] encounters go and abide by the outcome ... [and] no purpose except to make life easier for poets and revolutionaries' (CC, p. 13; cf. CIS, pp. 60–1).

As Fraser expresses it, Rorty's general approach in this mood is to invoke 'a version of the old trickle-down argument: liberty in the arts fosters equality in society; what's good for poets is good for workers, peasants and the hard-core unemployed' (AM, p. 308). But the complementarity position fails because 'to say goodbye to objectivity is not necessarily to say hello to a single, unitary solidarity; and because what's good for poets is not necessarily good for workers, peasants and the hard-core unemployed' (AM, p. 313).

2 The second 'opposition' position consists in the view that romanticism and pragmatism are antithetical to one another; that one has, in Fraser's words, 'to choose between the "sublime" cruelty of the strong poet and the beautiful "kindness" of the political reformer' (AM, p. 305). The chief point here is, as we have seen, that redescription can hurt, and in particular humiliate. In this mood Rorty wonders whether 'it is really possible to combine "the pleasures of

redescription" with sensitivity to "the sufferings of those being redescribed". He fears that the ironist demand for maximum cultural freedom may be elitist and [in particular] compatible with indifference to the sufferings of non-poets' (AM, p. 309). For we have seen that ironism is by definition reactive, feeding off a non-ironist public culture from which to be alienated. Ironism, even in a post-metaphysical culture, can only be the attitude of a stratum, a literary intelligentsia or cultural elite. Moreover, as we have seen, the ironist cannot claim that, in redescribing others, he is uncovering their true selves and interests, thereby empowering them. Furthermore, Rorty fears that 'behind the strong poet's love for what is original and wholly new lurks a secret contempt for what is familiar and widely shared' (AM, p. 309). Thus a philosophy for metaphor stands in stark contrast to a philosophy for politics.[7] On the romantic view, the social world exists for the sake of poets; on the pragmatist, poets exist for the sake of the social world. But the opposition position, like the complementarity position, fails because radical theory is not necessarily or always elitist, anti-democratic and at odds with collective concerns and political life (cf. AM, p. 313).

Before turning to Rorty's official reconciliation of (β) and (γ), let us consider in more detail Rorty's idea of an ironist. We have already seen that Rorty's notion of a 'final vocabulary' is suspect (p. 39 above). Such a vocabulary is final, it will be remembered 'in the sense that if doubt is cast on the worth of these words [e.g. "Christ", "decency", "England"], their user has no non-circular argumentative resource ... beyond them is only helpless passivity or a resort to force' (CIS, p. 73). An ironist:

(1) has radical and continuing doubts about the final vocabulary she currently uses ...;
(2) realizes that argument phrased in her present vocabulary can neither underwrite nor dissolve these doubts;
(3) in so far as she philosophizes about her situation, she does not think that her vocabulary is closer to reality than others (CIS, p. 73).

'Ironists see the choice between vocabularies as made ... simply by playing the new off against the old' (CIS, p. 73). This has two immediate consequences. First, it takes the choice out of 'the logical space of reasons' (PMN, pp. 182, 389). Secondly, it makes regression impossible by fiat. '[Ironists realize] that anything can be made to look good or bad by being redescribed' (CIS, p. 73). How about a famine, an earthquake or a stillborn child? Further, 'for us ironists, nothing can serve as a criterion of a final vocabulary save another such vocabulary; there is no answer to a redescription save a re-re-redescription' (CIS, p. 80). And a favourite polar contrast of Rorty's (criticized at p. 40 above): 'The ironist theorist distrusts the metaphysician's metaphor of a vertical view downward. He substitutes the historicist metaphor of looking back on the past along a horizontal axis' (CIS, p. 96). As Bernard Williams has put it: 'The liberal ironist commits himself to things while knowing that that is all he is doing; he believes in things while knowing, in a sense, that there is nothing to believe in.'[8] Such people are in a position that would be more aptly characterized as 'meta-unstable' than the Sartrian 'meta-stable' (CIS, p. 73). They are, at any rate, 'never quite able to take themselves seriously because always aware that the terms in which they describe themselves are subject to change, always aware of the contingency and fragility of their final vocabularies and thus of their selves' (CIS, pp. 73–4).

Two final points. First, is not the notion of a final vocabulary just emotivism writ large (and doesn't this place Rorty in a typical decisionist predicament)? Secondly, if the ironist is continually worried 'about the possibility that she has been initiated into the wrong tribe, taught to play the wrong language game' (CIS, p. 75), isn't this just to say that she wants to ask: 'Is ours a moral society?', which Rorty pronounces is a question we cannot ask (CIS, p. 59) (leading us into an ethnocentric predicament). That is to say, how is ironic doubt (worry or anxiety) possible? It would seem to be possible only from the outsider's point of view; but then this clashes with Rorty's ethnocentricism. More generally, we cannot simultaneously be at both insiders' (participants'/ethnocentric) and outsiders' (observers'/quasi-transcendent) points of view. Yet Rorty tends – in what we could dub the *Rorty flip* – to switch back and forth between one and another whenever it is rhetorically convenient. At the same time, his liberal ironist synthesis is always tending to split into an insider's liberal (about politics) and an outsider's ironist (about philosophy) schism.

3 The idea behind the separation position is, as Fraser points out, 'that two things that cannot be fused into one may nonetheless co-exist side by side, if clear and sharp boundaries are drawn between them' (AM, p. 311). Sublimity cannot be fused with decency, nor strong poetry with social responsibility. 'But if each were allotted its own sphere and barred from interfering with the other, then they might just make passably good neighbours' (AM, p. 311). In this third position – the official resolution of CIS – the ironist is to be restricted to the private domain, while the liberal is allocated the public terrain. In this way Rorty hopes to preserve both ecstasy and utility, 'the urge to think the unthinkable' and 'enthusiasm for the French Revolution'.[9]

The viability of the separation position depends on the feasibility of drawing a sharp and clear distinction between the private and public spheres. For as Charles Guignon and David Hiley put it: 'An individual's self-descriptions are realised in his or her agency in the public world, and public practices and institutions impact on the individual's capacities for self-fulfilment' (AM, p. 359).[10] Or, as Nancy Fraser expresses it: 'Final vocabularies do not neatly divide into public and private sectors; nor do actions neatly divide into private or public' (AM, p. 313). In particular, it is not possible to distinguish redescriptions that affect actions with consequences for others and those that do not (cf. AM, p. 312). Personal agency requires and uses social forms as its conditions, means and media and almost always has social consequences (including the reproduction or transformation of its own social structural prerequisites) (see PON, chapter 2;

RR, chapter 5). Intentional human agency is almost always other-oriented (under some description) and is always other-dependent. Tying one's shoelaces is also getting ready to go to work. Writing the perfect novel depends upon the work, skill and judgement of others (one's publishers, peers and descendants). Relationships, say, between men and women, or the employed and the unemployed, presumably fall within Rorty's private sector, and yet are clearly social, and as such legitimate topics for public political discussion and action. Even Derrida's 'private' allusions in works like *Envois*, much vaunted by Rorty in CIS, chapter 6, are not private as opposed to public: they are intended for a public, and they constitute precisely public-ations. Just as in PMN Rorty neglected the *materiality* of embodied human agency, so here in CIS he neglects the *sociality* of intentional human projects.

What has happened here is that a rough-and-ready distinction is being charged with the resolution of Rorty's dilemma. Yet the original terms of the dilemma and the ideological character of the distinction prevent any real clarification here. In the domain of the private sits the autonomized individual of classical philosophy. This is the space in which we are to come to terms with our 'aloneness' (PDP, p. 292). The privatized ironist, writing a diary no one can read, becomes the latest avatar of the lonely, doubting, Cartesian hero. On the other hand, in the domain of the public, reposes the official democratic polity, squeezing out social movements from trade unionism to feminism. Reified and hypostatized, the public realm becomes dislocated from the agency of the citizens who reproduce and transform the social structure – and only one political voice is heard: that of bourgeois-liberal democracy. On the one hand, singularity; on the other, technocracy. The untenability of Rorty's resolution is also revealed, as Fraser remarks, in the increasingly monological rather than poly-logical character of the concept of abnormal discourse employed. There is no longer a conversation with a multiplicity of voices, some commensurable, some not, but 'a solitary voice crying out into the night against an utterly undifferentiated background' (AM, p. 313).[11]

Rorty's privatized narcissistic conception of the radical has the consequence that both culture and theory get depoliticized. Moreover social space gets homogenized. 'In reaction against the extreme egotism and individualism of his conception of theory ... politics assumes an overly communitarian and solidary character.... Rorty assumes that there are no deep social cleavages capable of generating conflicting solidarities and opposing 'we's'.... Social engineering can replace political struggle.... Moreover with no deep rifts or pervasive axes of domination, practice can float free of theory.... Thus politics can be detheorized ... as theory becomes pure *poiesis* ... politics approaches pure *techne'* (AM, p. 315).

Fraser continues:

> It is paradoxical that such a dichotomous picture should be the upshot of a body of thought that aimed to soften received dichotomies.... It is also paradoxical that what was supposed to be a political polylogue comes increasingly to resemble a monologue.... Rorty makes non-liberal, oppositional discourses non-political by definition. Such discourses are associated by him with Romanticism, the quest for the uncharted.... Political discourse is implicitly deradicalized.... [It] is restricted to those who speak the language of bourgeois liberalism ... Rorty ends up supposing there is only one legitimate political vocabulary. (AM, pp. 315–6)

Thus, at CIS, p. 63, Rorty opines that 'Western social and political thought may have had the last *conceptual* revolution it needs.' Here, once again, Rorty fails to sustain the criterion of transformability in relation to social practices and discourses – the classic mistake of right-wing Hegelianism (cf. pp. 56 above). All politics is liberal politics; all theory is private. In any event, by dichotomizing private and public, singular individual and bourgeois community, Rorty cuts the ground from the possibility of radical transformative – putatively emancipatory – democratic politics (cf. AM, p. 316).

Underlying many of these aporiai lies the poverty of Rorty's conceptions of the 'social' and the 'moral'. What is the moral

constraint on the strong poet? Morality ceases to be conceived
as the voice of a divine or rational part of ourselves and comes
to be conceived as 'the voice of ourselves as members of a
community, speakers of a common language' (CIS, p. 59).
'The importance of this shift is it makes it impossible to ask
the question "Is ours a moral society?" It makes it impossible
to think that there is something which stands to my community
as my community stands to me, some larger community
called "humanity" which has an intrinsic nature. This shift is
appropriate for what Oakeshott calls a *societas* as opposed to
a *universitas*, to a society conceived as a band of eccentrics collaborating for purposes of mutual protection rather than a
band of fellow spirits united by a common goal' (CIS, p. 59).
Elsewhere, Rorty claims that anti-foundationalist pragmatism
shows us that 'what matters is our loyalty to other human
beings clinging together against the dark, not our hope of
getting things right' (CP, p. 166). This is a pretty whacky and
individualist conception of society – one appropriate to the
nuclear bunker. In any event, society is conceived here as a
group or collection of individuals, not as a structure, totality
or set of relationships. It also seems a pretty arbitrary group –
at least if it doesn't just mean 'the nation'.

'Morality', Rorty continues, 'is a matter of what Sellars calls
"we-intentions"' and 'the core meaning of "immoral action"'
is 'the sort of thing *we* don't do' (CIS, p. 59).[12] Rorty comments that 'this analysis takes the basic explanatory notion to
be "one of us"' (CIS, p. 190), and claims that 'the force of
"us" is, typically, contrastive in the sense that it contrasts
with a "they" which is also made up of human beings – the
wrong sort of human beings' (ibid.). He uses this analysis to
conjecture explanations as to why, if you were a Jew when the
trains were running to Auschwitz, your chances of being
hidden by your gentile neighbours were greater if you lived in
Denmark or Italy than in Belgium; and as to why Americans
might care more for the plight of young black Americans in
New York than those facing an equally hopeless life in the
slums of Manila or Dakar – they are fellow *Americans* (CIS,
p. 191). The role of the universalism common to Christian and

Kantian ethics and of abstractions such as 'humanity' is to provide us with an inspiring *focus imaginarius* to remind us to keep trying in a Fichtean way to expand our sense of 'us' as far as we can (CIS, pp. 195–6). This has the paradoxical conclusion that if we are completely successful, moral action, being contrastive, will no longer be possible – an isomorph of the paradox that Hegel saw afflicting Kantian ethics.

But there are a number of even more damaging difficulties with Rorty's account. First, its compatibility with irony, as I have already noted (p. 88 above), is in doubt. If irony involves awareness of the instability and contingency of our beliefs, how can we be prepared to 'stand for them unflinchingly' (CIS, p. 46). It would seem that *ceteris paribus* the more optional or contingent the belief, the weaker the grounds for acting on it. Secondly, if the only test for morality is the existence of a stable, well-adapted practice, then, as Hollis observes (AM, p. 249), slavery or fascism would have been justified. As for the future, Rorty says: 'It is quite possible that all such [liberal-democratic] institutions may vanish by the year 2100. There would then . . . be nothing to prevent the future being, as Orwell said, "a boot stamping on a human face, forever"' (TT, p. 567). Rorty continues: '*Nothing* is more important than the preservation of liberal institutions.' But what would Rorty's position be if he were not a member of a liberal society, but, say, of Pinochet's Chile or Franco's Spain? There would be a clear conflict between his insider's ethnocentricism and his outsider's but now transcendent liberalism. Presumably he would have to stick with the former.[13] As it is, as a member of his own society, Rorty is now prepared to modify criterion (β') (see p. 64 above): 'We have to insist that not every argument needs to be met in the terms in which it is presented. Accommodation and tolerance must stop short of a willingness to work within any vocabulary that one's interlocutor wishes to use, to take seriously any topic that he puts forward for discussion' (PDP, p. 290).

Third, Rorty's breakdown of the morality/prudence distinction (from CS/CIS, chapter 2 on) entails that all social questions are matters of praxiology, of social engineering. And for this

Rorty's 'we' has three convenient characteristics: (1) it is arbitrary (ungrounded and groundless), (2) it is flexible, (3) it is monolithic.

1 'In Sellars's account "intersubjective validity" can refer to validity for all members of the class of Milanese, or of New Yorkers, or of white males, or of ironist intellectuals, or of exploited workers' (CIS, p. 195). Or of 'bocce players' (CIS, p. 190), 'graduates of the class of '68'[14] or presumably 'wearers of purple socks'!

2 Surprisingly enough, Rorty's elastic 'we' operates to negate all difference. As Rebecca Comay has remarked: 'James and Dewey wait patiently at-the end of every road.'[15] '[Rorty's] "we" contracts or expands . . . to fit any available space.'[16] Thus: 'we liberal intellectuals' (HLP, p. 173); 'we heirs of the Enlightenment' (PDP, p. 288); 'we western liberal intellectuals' (SO, p. 23); 'we rich North American bourgeoisie' (PBL, p. 588); 'us . . . educated leisured policy-makers of the West' (CP, p. 203); 'us relatively leisured intellectuals, inhabiting a stable and prosperous part of the world' (PMN, p. 359); 'we . . . the people who have read and pondered Plato, Newton, Kant, Marx, Darwin, Freud, Dewey, etc.' (CP, p. 173); 'we liberal . . . searchers for a consensus' (SO, p. 12); 'we philosophy professors' (CP, p. 189); 'we Wittgensteinian nominalists' (DC, p. 189); and finally, 'we heirs to the historical contingencies which have created more and more cosmopolitan, more and more democratic political institutions' (CIS, p. 196). Opposed to this 'we' – encapsulating a spectrum from Daniel Bell to Jürgen Habermas – is a 'they' composed of 'theorists like Althusser, E. P. Thompson, Christopher Norris, Milton Fisk, Fred Jameson and so on' (TT, p. 569)!

3 But Rorty's we is not only elastic, it is pretty monolithic too. He shows little awareness of the conflicts within and between equally pressing solidarities (the stuff of 'moral dilemmas'); or of their inexplicitness and permeability. As Julian Bell complains: 'He doesn't tell us where "community" starts and stops. If we are South African whites, is apartheid part of our language and therefore not open to question? It

isn't: because we cannot effectively stop our ears to other languages than Boer intransigence claiming us for other communities – Christianity, Azania, etc. To carry any descriptive weight, Rorty's theory would have to allow for this contemporary experience, not confined to South Africa, of being dropped willy-nilly into a mish-mash of overlapping communities and moral claims that is in fact coterminus with "humanity".[17]

Next, Rorty says that morality 'has no automatic priority over ... private motives' (CIS, p. 194). But he leaves us without any clue as how to trade off public and private considerations. What if irony pulls one way and liberalism another? Finally, Rorty tells us that 'the conversation which it is our moral duty to continue is *merely* our project, the European intellectual's way of life ... [and that] *we do not know what "success" would mean except simply "continuance"'* (CP, p. 172). But it is not clear that Rorty can sustain the normativity of social life. For him, it would seem, criticism remains 'unserious'. However, 'ought we to go on as before?' and 'how are we to proceed?' remain vital and valid questions. These questions unasked and seemingly unaskable, Rorty proffers us nothing but an apologia for, and so eternalization (and divinization) of, the social status quo – quite contrary to the spirit of his intentions and the letter of his critique of epistemology (cf. PMN, pp. 9–10, 333n).

NOTES

1 T. Sorell, in AM, p. 24.
2 'On ethnocentrism: a reply to Clifford Geertz', *Michigan Quarterly Review* 25 (1986), pp. 533–4.
3 *Ordinary Vices*, Cambridge, Mass., 1984, pp. 43–8 and chapter 1 passim.
4 'Singularity and solidarity: Richard Rorty between Romanticism and technocracy', in AM, pp. 303–21.
5 Cf. Marx's '3rd Thesis on Feuerbach': 'The materialist doctrine concerning the changing of circumstances and upbringing forgets that circumstances are changed by men and that it is

essential to educate the educator himself. This doctrine must, therefore, divide society into two parts, one of which is superior to society.

The coincidence of the changing of circumstances and of human activity or self-changing can be conceived and rationally understood only as revolutionary practice' (*Early Writings*, ed. L. Colletti, Harmondsworth, 1975, p. 422).

6   *Guardian*, 23 June 1989, p. 25.

7   See R. Rorty, 'Philosophy as science, as metaphor and as politics', *The Institution of Philosophy: A Discipline in Crisis?*, ed. A. Cohen and M. Descal, La Salle, 1989.

8   'Getting it right', *London Review of Books*, 23 November 1989, p. 5.

9   R. Rorty, 'Habermas and Lyotard on postmodernity', *Habermas and Modernity*, ed. R. J. Bernstein, Cambridge, 1985, p. 175.

10 They add: 'It is the task of moral and social philosophy to clarify these bonds between civic responsibility and meaningful freedom' (ibid.).

11 Fraser adds: 'The only conceivable response to the voice is uncomprehending rejection or identificatory imitation. There is no room for a reply that could qualify as a different voice. There is no room for interaction' (AM, pp. 313–4); i.e. for conversation rather than dismissal or repetition.

12 See W. Sellars, *Science and Metaphysics*, London, 1968, chapters 6–7.

13 Cf. (1) 'Anti-anti-ethnocentrists suggest that liberals ... should simply drop the distinction between rational judgement and cultural bias' ('On ethnocentrism: a reply to Clifford Geertz', *Michigan Quarterly Review*, Summer 1986, pp. 525–34); (2) society must come to see that 'loyalty to itself is morality enough' (PBL, p. 585).

14 Cf. T. Eagleton, 'Defending the free world', *Socialist Register 1990*, ed. R. Miliband and L. Panitch, London, 1990.

15 'Interrupting the conversation: notes on Rorty', *Telos* 69 (Fall 1986), p. 129.

16 Ibid., pp. 120–1.

17 J. Bell, 'A liberal Utopia', *Times Literary Supplement*, 24 November 1989, p. 1246.

6

Rorty's Apologetics

We do not know what 'success' would mean except simply 'continuance'.

CP, p. 172

There is a structural factor tending to make Rorty unable to deal with the social phenomena of criticism, critique and (non-incommensurable) change, lending his work to an apologia for, and so normalization, and thence eternalization (and so divinization), of the social status quo. On empirical realism, identifying the realms of experience and the real, intellectual or poetic change, or even dissent, is tantamount to a breakdown in the uniformity of nature! (Cf. RTS, p. 163.) This renders any generalizations impossible (they are immediately falsified). So the empirical realist tendency is to say, with Hume, that 'mankind are ... much the same in all times and places'[1] (cf. SR, p. 289), or with Rorty that 'we do not know what "success" would mean except simply "continuance"' (CP, p. 172), or alternatively to deny the existence of any pattern at all (or assert the occurrence of chaos – cf. Rorty's disjunctive dilemmas).

At any rate, in the political domain Rorty's apologetic intent is pretty clear. 'Bourgeois liberalism' is 'the best example of ... solidarity yet achieved' (CP, p. 207). 'We should be more

willing than we are to celebrate bourgeois capitalist society as
the best polity actualized so far, while regretting that it is
irrelevant to most of the problems for most of the population
of the planet' (CP, p. 210, n. 16). 'There seems no particular
reason why, after dumping Marx, we have to keep repeating
all the nasty things about bourgeois liberalism he taught
us to say' (CP, p. 207). In CC, Rorty actually describes his
position as apologetic, defining apologetics as 'a way of describing old institutions and practices in a new and more
useful way' (CC, p. 10; cf. CIS, pp. 56–7), arguing that it
presents 'a circular justification of our practices', which
'makes one feature of our culture look good by citing still
another' (CC, p. 13).

As Bernstein notes, there is a disturbing proto-positivism in
Rorty's work (OSF, p. 544). This surfaces in two ways: in his
rejection of theory in politics; and in his rejection of any
concept of human subjectivity. I shall discuss the former
mainly in the present section; and the latter mainly in the
next. Thus he writes: 'Whether Soviet imperialism is a
threat is a paradigm of a non-"ideological", unphilosophical,
straightforwardly empirical, question. It is a question about
what will happen if such-and-such other things happen (if
NATO collapses, if South America goes communist and so
on)' (TT, pp. 578–9, n. 25). 'Such questions' are not to be
'answered by improving one's philosophical sophistication'
but rather by, say, 'reading intelligence reports on what the
Politburo and the Soviet generals have been saying to one
another lately' (ibid.). Theory and theory-ladenness dis-
appear. Such fetishized facts accompany the autonomized individuals assumed (in different ways) in both liberal and ironist
theory to replicate classically the contours of the positivist
problematic (cf. SR. chapter 3.3; and RR, chapter 4). And in
those fetishized facts Rorty comes very close to replacing social for natural foundations of knowledge – an historical for an
epistemological myth of the given (cf. OSF, p. 551).

Rorty also expresses a proto-positivism in his unequivocal
rejection of any concept of human subjectivity. The human
being, he insists, is 'a network of beliefs, desires and emotions

with nothing behind it – no substrate behind the attributes. For purposes of moral and political deliberation and conversation, a person just *is* that network, as for purposes of ballistics she is a point-mass, or for purposes of chemistry a linkage of molecules' (PBL, pp. 585–6). This is Rorty the Quinean epistemological behaviourist. He goes on to remark: 'Irrationality, in both physics and ethics, is a matter of behaviour that leads one to abandon, or be stripped of, membership in some such community' (PBL, p. 586). But of course, it makes no sense to talk of the rationality$_{id}$ of point-masses or molecules, as distinct from our discourse about them. Rorty's undifferentiated hyper-naturalism (coupled with his transitive–intransitive confusion) has let him down again here.

This is in a celebrated/notorious article called 'Postmodernist bourgeois liberalism'.[2] Jo Burrows has remarked that: 'Liberals can afford to be complacent about liberal foundations and (thereby) deconstruct "the tradition"; that is "put less value on being in touch with reality" (PMN, p. 365). They have already reaped its intellectual fruits'(AM, p. 336, n. 23). Sandra Harding makes a similar point. She asks: 'Should feminists be willing to give up the political benefits which can come from believing that we are producing a new, less biased, more accurate social science? ... Is it premature for women to be willing to give up what they have never had.... Perhaps only those who have had access to the benefits of the Enlightenment can "give up" those benefits.'[3]

Richard Bernstein has isolated three main motifs in Rorty's 'kibitzing' since PMN. First, his continuing campaign against (real or imaginary) fundamentalism (discussed in chapter 2 and to be returned to in Part IV), especially realism; second, his poeticism (discussed in chapters 3 and 5); and third, his defence of 'postmodernist bourgeois liberalism' (OSF, pp. 541–2). Rorty's defence of liberalism has seemed to many to be little more than an apologia for the status quo – the very type of liberalism that Dewey judged to be 'irrelevant and doomed' (cf. OSF, p. 541).[4] Indeed Rorty's present position seems to consist in a combination of radical, chic, postmodernist playfulness, taking up the burden of Rorty's romantic impulse, and old-fashioned cold war liberalism, discharging the residue of Rorty's pragmatic impulse. Rorty is sensitive to the charge that his recent writings adopt an 'air of light-minded aestheticism ... towards traditional philosophical questions' (PDP, p. 293). His defence of it is that, like the rise of large market economies, 'such philosophical superficiality and light-mindedness helps along the disenchantment of the world. It helps make the world's inhabitants more pragmatic, more tolerant, more liberal, more receptive to the appeal of instrumental rationality' (ibid.). Rorty's commitment to Weberian *Zweckrationalität*, at least in the form of technocracy, social engineering, is evident here.[5]

It has seemed to many that there is something too facile about Rorty's debunking of 'the spirit of seriousness'. As Bernstein points out:

> One reason that the 'classical' pragmatism of Peirce, Dewey, Mead and James went into eclipse is because many thinkers began to feel that the pragmatic attempt to soften and blur all philosophical distinctions had the unfortunate consequence of depriving us of the analytical tools needed for clarifying and getting a grip on important differences that make a difference, and resulted in a bland undifferentiated monotonous holism. Rorty ... is guilty of a similar tendency of levelling in his light-minded joshing. (OSF, p. 543)

In short, Rorty neglects differences that make a difference (*contra* CP, p. xxix; cf. p. 7 above). We could call this levelling tendency the '*Rorty roller*'. It ties in with Rorty's tendency to negate all difference noted in chapter 5 (p. 94). It does not follow that just because a line (say, between the necessary and the contingent) is fuzzy and changeable in particular places that clear paradigm instances of positions either side of the line cannot be demonstrated.

In PDP, Rorty, espousing what he calls a 'Deweyan histori-cist interpretation' of Rawls' theory of justice, defends Rawls against his so-called 'communitarian' critics, and in particular against those criticisms advanced by Sandel in *Liberalism and the Limits of Justice.*[6] Rorty's position is that liberal democracy does not need a philosphical justification. To this end he disentangles three strands or claims in communitarianism:

1 The empirical prediction that no society that sets aside the idea of ahistorical truth ... can survive (PDP, p. 281).
2 The moral judgement that liberal societies produce undesirable types of human beings (PDP, pp. 281–2).[7]
3 The claim that political institutions 'presuppose' a doctrine about human beings and that such a doctrine must ... make clear the essentially historical character of the self (PDP, p. 282).

To evaluate this third claim, Rorty poses two questions. The first (a) is 'whether there is any sense in which liberal democracy "needs" philosophical justification at all' (PDP, p. 282). The second (b) is 'whether a conception of the self which, as Taylor says, makes "the community constitutive of the individual"[8] does in fact comport better with liberal democracy than does the Enlightenment conception of the self' (PDP, p. 282). Rorty goes on:

> I can preview what is to come by saying that I shall answer 'no' to the first question about the communitarian's third claim and 'yes' to the second. I shall be arguing that ... liberal democracy can get along without philosophical presuppositions.... But I shall also argue that a conception of the self which makes the community constitutive of the self does comport well with liberal democracy. (PDP, p. 283)

Note that Rorty makes clear that nothing very much hangs on the answer to (b):

> for purposes of liberal social theory, one can do without such a model [of the self (as a centreless web of conditioned beliefs and desires)].... If, however, one has a taste for philosophy – if one's vocation, one's private pursuit of perfection, entails constructing models of such entities as 'the self' ... one *will* want a picture of the self. Since my own vocation is of this sort,

and the moral identity around which I wish to build such models is that of a citizen of a liberal-democratic state, I commend the picture of the self as a centreless and contingent web to those with similar tastes and similar identities. But I would not commend it to those with a similar vocation but dissimilar moral identities ... (PDP, pp. 291-2)

It is on (a) that Rorty wishes to concentrate.

But before I get on to that, it is worth comparing (1) and (2) with two objections – which I shall label (4) and (5) – Rorty considers in CIS: 'The social glue holding together the ideal liberal society described in the previous chapter consists in little more than a consensus that the point of social organization is to let everybody have a chance of self-creation to the best of his or her abilities, and that that goal requires, besides peace and wealth, the standard "bourgeois freedoms"' (CIS, p. 84). 'The first [objection] is that as a practical matter the glue is just not thick enough – that the (predominantly) metaphysical rhetoric of public life in the democracies is essential to the continuation of free institutions.' But the decline of religious faith has not weakened but strengthened liberal societies; so by analogy, a decline in metaphysical beliefs may do the same – either have no or a positive impact (CIS, p. 85ff). 'The second [objection] is that it is psychologically impossible to be a liberal ironist' (CIS, p. 85; cf. p. 88). The liberal ironist thinks 'that recognition of a common susceptibility to humiliation is the *only* social bond that is needed' (CIS, p. 91); 'she thinks that what unites her with the rest of the species is not a common language but *just* susceptibility to pain and in particular to that special sort of pain which the brutes do not share with the humans – humiliation' (CIS, p. 92). 'What matters for the liberal ironist is not finding [a reason to care about suffering] but making sure that she *notices* suffering when it occurs' (CIS, p. 93). 'For the liberal ironist skill at imaginative identification does the work which the liberal metaphysician would like to have done by a specifically moral motivation' (ibid.).

The metaphysician's association of theory with social hope and of literature with private perfection is, in an ironist culture, reversed. Within a liberal metaphysical culture the disciplines which were charged with penetrating behind the many private appearances to the one general common reality – theology, science, philosophy – were the ones which were expected to bind human beings together; and thus to help eliminate cruelty. Within an ironist culture, by contrast, it is the disciplines which specialise in thick descriptions of the private and the idiosyncratic which are assigned this job. In particular, novels and ethnographies which sensitize one to the pain of those who do not speak our language must do the job which demonstrations of a common human nature were supposed to do. (CIS, p. 94)

For Rorty the chief point *re* 3(a) is this: 'As citizens and as social theorists we can be as indifferent to philosophical disagreements about the nature of the self as Jefferson was to theological differences about the nature of God' (PDP, p. 285). Rorty thinks that liberal democracy does not need a philosophical justification. But the model of philosophical justification he appears to be operating with is – once more – an overly simplistic one: as consisting in deduction from unassailable premises about human nature or the self. At the same time, he thinks that it is translucently clear what we mean by 'liberalism', thus falling into an essentialist mode of speech and overlooking the historical fact that we are confronted with conflicting and incompatible interpretations and practices in 'liberal democracy' (cf. OSF, p. 549). As Bernstein notes, while arguing that disciplines cannot be conceived as 'natural kinds', he writes as if philosophy – and even politics – is a natural kind (cf. OSF, pp. 547–8). He tends to operate with the dichotomy that we must either (α) appeal to what is local and ethnocentric, or (β) appeal to fixed permanent ahistorical foundations (OSF, p. 550).[9] At times Rorty appeals to our intuitions – as if they did not conflict; and to the method of 'reflective equilibrium', as if it were an algorithm for the resolution of conflicting intuitions. In all this Rorty glosses

over, as Bernstein says, 'what appears to be the overwhelming "fact" of contemporary life – the breakdown of moral and
political consensus and the conflicts and incompatibility
among competing social practices' (OSF, p. 552). Moreover, 'it
is never clear why Rorty, who claims that there is no consensus about competing conceptions of the good life, thinks there
is any more consensus about conceptions of justice or liberal
democracy' (ibid.). Rorty also tends to downplay what has
become a major problem for liberals, viz. 'the disparity between the "ideals" of liberty and equality that liberals profess
and the actual state of affairs in so-called liberal societies'
(OSF, p. 552). Nor does Rorty face up to the challenge posed
by Marx in his critique of ideology. He dismisses this notion
in two footnotes in CIS (at CIS, pp. 59n, 84n). Bernstein also
makes the *ad hominem* point that 'sometimes it seems as if
what Rorty means by "we" are "all those who agree with
me"' (OSF, p. 554) – a projection of me. One could also
usefully contrast Gadamerian hermeneutics constrained by
acknowledgement of the existence of an 'other' (OSF, pp.
554–5; cf. PON 1, pp. 200–2; PON 2, pp. 156–8) with Rorty –
for whom 'there never seems to be any constraints on me and
my interpretations.' This is the difference between the objective idealist and the strong misreader (CP, chapter 8 – especially p. 151): 'The critic asks neither the author nor the text
about their intentions but simply beats the text into a shape
which will serve his own purposes' (ibid.).

Rorty seems clearly enough to be *arguing* against all notions
of a centred and transcendental self. He cannot just say that a
theory of the self is optional – for the locus of controversial
reflective theories or pictures is *not* in grounding political
convictions on firm foundations but in *specifying* and *describing*
what precisely we mean by liberalism and liberal democracy
(OSF, p. 557; cf. also SR, p. 207). The history of philosophy
that underlines Rorty's critique of foundationalism is powerful
but clichéd. Is there a sense in which repeated application of
Rorty's disjunctive dilemmas reveals him as a disappointed
absolutist? One must wonder whether his lightminded
aestheticism serves merely to disguise this. As Bernstein
puts it:

'Rorty, who has eloquently called for open conversation, fails to realize how his rhetorical strategies tend to close off serious/playful conversation about liberalism and democracy' (OSF, p. 560).

There is evidence, as Charles Guignon and David Hiley argue, that Rorty's moral concerns that surface near the end of PMN drive the argument of the book as a whole (cf. PMN, p. 377). Moreover, Rorty's anti-fundamentalism is evident as early as LT (cf. p. 39). Rorty's anti-fundamentalist pragmatism is designed to avoid the tendency to the 'dehumanization of human beings' (PMN, p. 377) in traditional fundamentalist philosophy. It shows us that, in a typical Rorty disjunct, 'what matters is our loyalty to other human beings clinging together against the dark, not our hope of getting things right' (CP, p. 166). Rorty's emphasis is on objectivity not so much as being *defined* in terms of intersubjective validity/consensus/solidarity – the classic neo-Kantian move – but as being *replaced* by it.

What is Rorty's conception of the self, then? As Guignon and Hiley put it: 'We exist as, so to speak, intersections of transient public interpretations' (AM, p. 344). 'There is nothing which "has" these interpretations ... we are interpretations all the way down' (AM, pp. 344–5). That is to say, 'we are what we [or others] say'.[10] For Rorty this helps to dispel the non-textualist illusion 'that deep down beneath all the texts, there is something which is not just one more text but that to which various texts are trying to be "adequate"' (CP, p. xxxvii). Rorty's characterization of the self reflects the trend towards decentring the subject (PON 1, pp. 142–6; PON 2, pp. 111–14). For Rorty, for the 'purposes of moral and political deliberation and conversation, a person just is ... a network of beliefs, desires and emotions with nothing behind it – no substrate behind the attributes' (PBL, pp. 585–6) – 'a network that is constantly re-weaving itself ... in the hit-or-miss way in which cells readjust to the pressures of the environment' (PBL, p. 586).

To understand ourselves as self-reweaving webs of beliefs and desires is to understand that the best stance to take towards ourselves is 'a spirit of playfulness and irony' (CS,

p. 14). But, as we have seen, Rorty rejects the *ressentiment* against the bourgeoisie found in Nietzsche, Sartre and Foucault. On the contrary, for Rorty, we have every reason to 'celebrate bourgeois capitalist society as the best polity actualised so far' (CP, p. 210n) and to dedicate ourselves to realizing that society's ideals while rejecting its pretensions to transcendental grounding. We have already referred to Rorty's breakdown of the traditional morality/prudence distinction as at best 'the difference between an appeal to the interests of the community and an appeal to our private, possibly conflicting, interests' (CC, p. 12). Rorty distinguishes private morality, the 'private ethic of self creation' from public morality, the 'public ethic of mutual accommodation'. The key figure in defining the issues of private morality for our age is Freud. In FMR Rorty distinguishes three ways of seeing the self. The traditional view of the self as centred comes to be replaced by the view of the self as a centreless machine. What Freud adds to the mechanized view of the self is the suggestion that there are different 'quasi-selves' or 'persons' within us who are causing us to do things. As Guignon and Hiley report it, 'drawing on Davidson's reading of Freud, Rorty claims that if we think of a person as a "coherent and plausible set of beliefs and desires", then it will be natural to think that our bodies play host to "two or more persons", who enter into causal relations with one another; though "they do not, normally, have conversational relations"'(FMR. pp. 4–5) (AM, p. 351).

According to Rorty this Freudian picture of the self transforms our moral self-understanding and in particular frees us up to interpret ourselves in any way we like. And this in turn points to a new character ideal. This character ideal Rorty calls the ideal of self-enlargement. This aesthetic ideal is illustrated by de Sade, Byron and Hegel in the fields of sexual experimentation, politics and language, respectively. It is opposed to the traditional ascetic ideal of self-purification, whose mode is tragic rather than comic and to the hermeneutical ideal of self-focusing. Freud helps us to 'think of moral reflection and sophistication as a matter of self-creation rather than self-knowledge' (FMR, p. 12). Freud's 'major legacy' is the 'in-

creased ability of the syncretic, ironic, nominalist intellectual'
to play with 'religious, moral, scientific, literary, philosophical
and psychoanalytical vocabularies without asking the question
"And which of these shows us how things *really* are?"' (FMR,
p. 15). Moreover, a laid-back attitude to ourselves can be
combined with a less judgemental attitude towards others.
Thus we can see the 'Kantian dutiful fulfiller of universal
obligations' and the playful Nietzschean experimentalist as
'exemplifying two out of many forms of adaptation, two out
of many strategies for coping with the contingencies of one's
upbringing' (CS, p. 12). Freud democratized genius by showing us how to see every human being as having a creative
unconscious. Freud taught us how to see every human life as
a poem, how to see sexual perversion, extreme cruelty or
obsession as the private poem of the pervert, the sadist or the
lunatic (CS, p. 14). And Rorty clearly believes that a private
morality dedicated to self-enlargement comports better with
our liberal, democratic ideals.

However, there are at least four difficulties in Rorty's vision
of a culture devoted to the spirit of playfulness and irony.
There is the question as to whether it would not exacerbate
rather than dissolve the disorders of the self that psychiatrists
have been reporting recently (see AM, p. 356). Secondly,
there is the worry that it would obliterate the distinction
between manipulative and non-manipulative social relations;
and thirdly, even encourage the development of undesirable
character types. Rorty replies to this objection by saying that
'if we [content] ourselves with narratives tailored *ad hoc* to the
contingencies of individual lives, then we may welcome a
Baconian culture dominated by "the Rich Aesthete, the Manager and the Therapist" – not necessarily as the final goal of
human progress, but at least as a considerable improvement
on cultures dominated by the Warrior or the Priest' (FMR, pp.
17–18). Finally, there is still the split in the self – between the
self who is the web or machine and the self who reweaves the
web or programmes the machine; and the associated difference between the vocabularies we must use in talking of
ourselves as machines for the purposes of prediction and

control and as moral or conversational agents. The reweaving self must be at least as real (and as active and as emergent) as is required for the agency necessary for sustaining Rortian conversation – or better, abnormal discourse. Linked to this split between the self who is the web and the self who reweaves the web are splits between the existentialist and communitarian selves, the monologic and polylogic selves and the self as *en-soi* and as *pour-soi*. Rorty has not overcome the antinomies that flawed the work of Kant and of Sartre.

NOTES

1 D. Hume, *An Enquiry Concerning Human Understanding*, Oxford, 1963, p. 8.
2 By the time of TT and CIS he has renounced, under the influence of Habermas's *The Philosophical Discourse of Modernity* Cambridge, 1986, any formal postmodernist allegiances (see TT, p. 578, n. 22).
3 S. Harding, in *Feminism and Methodology*, ed. S. Harding, Milton Keynes, 1987, pp. 188–9. Cf. also S. Lovibond, 'Feminism and democracy', *New Left Review* 178 (1989).
4 'If radicalism be defined as perception of the need for radical change, then today any liberalism which is not also radicalism is irrelevant and doomed', J. Dewey, 'Liberalism and social action', *The Philosophy of John Dewey*, ed. J. McDermott, New York, 1973, p. 648, cited in OSF, p. 540.
5 Marx and Weber both argued (in different ways) that its spread undermined the very social conditions required for individual autonomy and freedom. But Rorty does not take up their challenge.
6 Cambridge, 1982.
7 Such as MacIntyre's 'Rich aesthete, manager and therapist', see *After Virtue*, London, 1981, chapter 3 and passim.
8 C. Taylor, *Philosophical Papers*, Vol. 2, Cambridge, 1985, p. 8.
9 Cf. R. Comay, 'Interrupting the conversation: Notes on Rorty', *Telos* 69 (1986), p. 124: 'Observe the gentle blackmail. Either we celebrate our own society as the best of all conceivable worlds or we reveal our own essentialist stripes' (cf. chapter 1, p. 20).
10 Cf. J. Rée, 'Timely meditations', *Radical Philosophy* 55 (1990), p. 34.

Part IV

Kibitzing

7

Reference, Fictionalism and Radical Negation

Few areas of philosophical contestation generated as much heat during the years in which Rorty was composing PMN as the theory of reference. It is, therefore, unsurprising that Rorty should have decided it was a suitable object for his kibitzing.[1] Rorty has dual philosophical interests here:

1 He wants to critique linguistified forms of foundationalism.
2 He wants to obliterate any philosophically significant differences between factual and fictional discourse to bolster his deflationary account of science and the other 'hard' disciplines – in both cases the narrator is just 'telling a story', not reflecting the world (cf. CP, p. 110).

Sometimes he attributes sceptical/fundamentalist ambitions to both the descriptivist (Frege, Russell, Strawson, Searle) and the essentialist (Kripke, Putnam, Donellan) parties to the dispute (e.g. PMN, pp. 293–4); at other times merely to the latter (e.g. PMN, p. 289). Rorty's main animus in the case of both his interests is to argue that reference is a 'pointless . . . philosopher's notion' (CP, p. 127), 'a term of philosophical art' (PMN, p. 289). All that we require are the ordinary notion of 'talking about' plus a diagnostic or corrective notion of 'really talking about' where we situate a speaker's utterances in the context of our own greater or new knowledge or beliefs.

In TM, pp. 324ff, Rorty distinguishes three types or concepts of reference. Reference$_1$ or talking about is 'a purely "intentional" relation which can hold between an expression and a non-existent object.' It is a 'common-sensical notion' (PMN, p. 289). On it 'you refer to what you think you are referring to' (TM, p. 324). Reference$_3$ is 'a factual relation which holds between an expression and some other portion of reality whether anybody knows it holds or not'. It satisfies the axiom of existence, AE: 'whatever is referred to must exist' (CP, p. 111).[2] Reference$_2$ is an intermediate notion which enables us to correct what we take to be the misguided attempts of a speaker to refer to antiquated theoretical entities or to non-existents. As Vision puts it, précising Rorty (TM, pp. 325–6): 'Operating with reference$_2$ we may expect to hear remarks such as: "When the Greeks spoke of Zeus' thunderbolts they were *really* referring to electrical discharges." On reference$_3$ the Greeks would have failed to refer, while on *talking about* they would have referred to Zeus' thunderbolts' (AM, p. 84). Or, in another commentator's words,[3] 'A is what one really talks about if it is as a result of mistaking A [e.g. electrical discharges] for B [Zeus' thunderbolts (caloric, phlogiston, etc.)] that one makes a reference, or putative reference, to B; or if it is to A to which one would have had to refer in order to have said something literally true.'

I want to distinguish at the outset 'conversational reference' – c ref – and 'practical reference' – p ref. *Conversational referring* is a human, quasi-deictic act by which, with any means to hand, one person tries to draw the attention of another to a being, event, etc. c ref is governed by conventions, such as those that underpin the institution of 'naming' and is primarily oriented to communicative success, including communicative success in the transitive dimension of scientific life. But such an act may be to a being whether it is present or not; it may be more or less communicatively successful; and the verbal means may be semantically incorrect or attributively false. *Practical referring* is a human, quasi-deictic act by means of which one or more person achieves a physical relationship or link with some being, event, etc., which may have been previously more or less hidden or undetected. p ref is what is achieved in the existential discoveries, displays and demonstrations in the intransitive dimension of scientific life. 'Epistemic access'[4] involves practical reference, and practical reference may involve capturing or landing on or revealing or photographing something,[5] temporarily or permanently (indefinitely) securing access either (a) to the denotation or (b) to some effect(s) of the denotation of a term. (a) and (b) correspond respectively to our perceptual and causal criteria for attributing reality to things, etc. (cf. PON 1, pp. 15–16; PON 2, p. 12). p ref presupposes that the being, event, etc. has already been known and conversationally referred to, e.g. as a hypothetical, postulated or imagined entity in theoretical science, under some identifying description and before any baptism could occur. p ref, when secured, satisfies a modified form of the axiom of existence – what I will call the axiom of reality, AR: 'whatever is p referred to must be real.' Thus something may be absent from its space–time region and so be non-existent in this sense, and yet this absence, precisely *qua* absense, may be real in virtue of its causal powers – the case of what I will call *radical negation* – and be p referred to. c ref (e.g. in the hypothetical or fictional modes) need not satisfy the axiom of reality.

Whether the essentialist or the entire theory of reference is enmeshed in a Cartesian-sceptical-foundationalist problematic, it is clear that Rorty's favoured 'reference$_1$' is. For what could be more fundamentalist, dogmatic and non-fallibilist (as well as in keeping with the spirit of identity theory) than a notion on which thinking one is φ'ing and φ'ing amount to one and the same thing, one on which thinking that one is referring to x guarantees that one is? This constitutes a level of self-certifying reference, comparable to Russell's logically proper names, or the phenomenalist reconstruction of reality (cf. SR, chapter 3.3–5), effacing the distinctions between the real, the imagined and the imaginary, between brute fabrications – which I shall call 'ficts' – and facts. Is this not the super-idealist (see SR, chapter 1.1) mirror-image of the positivist ontic fallacy, on which what is one refers to, namely what one refers to, is? If I refer to a shadow on the wall as a person, or to electrical discharges as Zeus' thunderbolts, then what I say will be either false or unassessable so that, just as to make sense of the falsification of existential claims in science, we need the notion of something like c or p referential$_{id}$ failure and hence something like reference$_3$, the 'philosopher's notion'. Two further considerations point in the same direction. First, intention in referential failure may be indeterminate – as in the sort of case Vision gives where someone asks: 'How can Francis Bacon have had time to paint so many canvasses and write so many philosophy books?', where the speaker is so thoroughly confused that he could not sincerely say *which* of the two (relevant) Francis Bacons he was enquiring about (AM, p. 89). Secondly, pragmatically it is difficult to see how the transition from 'talking about' to 'really talking about' could occur, except via the failure of reference$_3$ – as reported in some such remark as 'Zeus doesn't exist (or cause thunderbolts)'.

But does the new essentialist or causalist approach guarantee or underscore the truth of our judgements? On the contrary, as Houghton remarks, 'it seems to be a consequence of causal theories ... that all our claims could turn out to be false, taken literally as claims about the stated referent, whereas on descriptivist theories [which Rorty favours (TM, p. 330)] some of our claims, if not most of them, would have to be true for them to be claims about anything' (AM, p. 158). The new theory does not imply that our words are bound to refer. It is allowed that the history of a name may end in a 'block' (Donellan); and that there may be nothing to which the name was given in an initial act of dubbing. Nor does the indexical theory of natural kind terms guarantee reference. If there are paradigms for the terms, there can be no assurance that they exemplify a or the same kind. Rorty caricatures essentialist theories as attempts to substitute the purely natural or factual for conventional or intentional relations. But the intention to preserve reference, as Houghton points out (AM, p. 159), plays a crucial part in Kripke's account, which is best seen precisely as an attempt to uncover the conventions governing the reference of proper names. Similarly, if the application of a natural kind term is determined by the underlying nature or real essence of paradigm cases, 'that can only be because it is now a feature of the socially accepted uses of that word that its application be determined in that way'.[6]

Moreover, as Houghton notes (AM, p. 161), Rorty's alternative apparatus lets him down at the very point where he thinks the philosophical notion is at its most counterintuitive, viz. in discourse about fictional characters. For the idea that in order to refer to a fictional character intention suffices is as unacceptable as in the case of a historical person. Thus 'Hamlet's wife' fails to refer, just as surely as the 'present King of France' does. Moreover many Kripkean insights can be carried over here. For instance, if one can refer to Napoleon knowing about him only that he was defeated at Waterloo, so one can refer to Juliet knowing only that she is a character in a Shakespeare play. And if a whole community of scholars can be in error about who a certain historical figure was, say the real Thales, so it can be in error about the identity of particular literary characters. Thus, to take Houghton's example, relying on information supplied by some ancient commentator, we may believe falsely that Archipelagos was a buffoon in one of Aristophanes' lost comedies, whereas he was really a character from a play by a rival comedian. Rorty seems mistaken in thinking that if one wants a theory of (conversational) reference which permits reference to fictional characters, 'the cluster-concept view will be one's choice' (TM, p. 330). Sentences like 'Hamlet was a bachelor' can be treated as implicitly intensional contexts with some prefix such as 'in the story/ play ...' being understood and ready to be made explicit in the event of misunderstanding (cf. AM, p. 162). As Vision suggests (AM, p. 85), should the realist want to maintain that there are truths about fictional non-existents, there are a number of possibilities – e.g. an appeal to the ground of 'fictional facts' in something non-fictional (e.g. an event involving an author) and/or the acceptance of fictional truths in social reality. Thus the condition that fictions have real, not fictional, causes may serve as a basis for tracing references to fictional characters to appropriate termini (cf. AM, p. 99, n. 33).

For Rorty, semantics cannot tell us anything about how words relate to the world, 'for there is nothing *general* to be said' (CP, p. 127). But, as Houghton says, it does not follow from this 'that the reference of a name neither can be, nor has to be, determined in advance of establishing the meaning and truth-value of sentences containing the name' (AM, p. 164).

According to Kripke,[7] the reference of a name is determined by a chain of communication stretching back from current uses of the name to an original act of baptism in which something was first assigned the name. The reference of the name is ultimately fixed by the identity – and very being – of the thing upon which it was initially conferred. Such a theory has the virtue of being able to cope with certain intuitions with which descriptivist theories are unable to cope – for example, that we may be quite mistaken about who the real Thales was, or in thinking that it was Gödel who invented Gödel's theorem, or about the identity of the author of Shakespeare's plays.

The problem, however, with Kripke's theory is that, if it were true, then we ought to have no less difficulty in supposing that we might be as radically mistaken about which planet is the real Venus. And this is not so. For names play a role in the existence$_{id}$ and history$_{id}$ of people and some other things too – such as the proper names given to human artefacts such as towns, roads, shops and brands of manufactured goods – that they do not play in the case of things in the purely natural world. In fact, there is a continuum from personal names and artefacts through the socialized parts of nature (pets, forests, the Grand Canyon) to the variably socially affecting parts of nature (think of the quasi-baptismal dubbing of hurricanes) to the praxis-independent or neutral parts of nature. But even in the latter case the second planet has its conventional name and a justification must be given for a departure from it; just as a justification must be given for any departure from the use of 'copper' to say 'reppoc' or 'tin' to refer to copper. Still 'Venus' is not part of the history of Venus. It is part of the history$_{td}$ of (astronomical) names; whereas 'Aristotle' and to a lesser extent 'Fido' are also part of the history$_{id}$ of the things named. As Houghton puts it: 'A person has a name which he recognizes as his own and what that name is becomes as much a fact about him as his birthplace and nationality, and is as important to his identity as they are' (AM, p. 164). A general convention N now becomes available. The name that a person answers to and so on is his 'real' name, and he is the right referent of his name. Breaches of this convention – calling Androulla 'Antigone' – result in referential$_{id}$ failure. It is not only personal names but humanized places, artefacts, and so on along the continuum to which these considerations apply. Thus 'if my name is a fact about me, so the names of New York, Red Square, the Old Kent Road and Harrods are facts about them and resonant parts of their history' (AM, p. 165). Of course, persons and places can undergo changes of name, or can possess several names, including different names for different phases or contexts of their life (stage-names, pen-names, transsexuals, split, changing and multiple personalities/identities). But name changes or differences that occur within the living history of a person or the inhabited working history of a place, etc. must not be confused with changes of belief that occur as a result of mistakes – e.g. calling New York 'Washington' – in the writing of historical records. This would be to confuse the role of proper names in the history$_{id}$ of persons and places with their role in historical discourse (or writing)$_{td}$ about persons and places.

These considerations both explain our intuitions to which Kripkeans appeal and expose the limits of such theories. For it is only when a thing can be said to have a *real name*, a name that is part of its history, that the original application, the baptism or whatever, can be supposed to have endowed the thing with its real name, and so only then will the original application be of sufficient significance to regulate later uses of the name as a referring expression. Houghton also regards these considerations as calling into question the need for the further element in the Kripkean theory, namely the idea of a chain of communication in which referential links are preserved between earlier and later uses of the name. For so far as things may be said to have and bear names independently of those names being used to refer to them, then a later user's use of a right name to refer to a thing need not depend on his being party to any such chain of communication. If he refers to the correct referent by the use of that referent's real name (i.e. if he refers to the being named as X by 'X'), then the question of any, let alone an exactly right, chain of communication becomes irrelevant from the point of view of the success of reference, remaining relevant only for giving grounds that the person was so named, that the reference is correct. But the success of an act is not to be confused with its justification. As Houghton expresses it: 'how we know the meaning is one thing, what the meaning is is another' (AM, p. 167). Still, it seems difficult to see how people could get the name right except via some such – perhaps very attenuated (the conference badge, credit card, amulet or epitaph) – chain of communication. And the chain might be vital for disambiguation: 'which Antigone (Socrates/Rorty/Latifa)?'

Houghton concludes from this that there is 'good reason for being sceptical about the possibility of a theory of the reference of proper names which is both general and substantive' (AM, p. 167). Rorty is quite right in saying that in answering questions about what people have in mind, we become involved in matters of 'expository or historiographical convenience' where 'nothing but tact and imagination will do' (PMN, p. 293). But this is not to say that 'to what does the name "p" refer?' – any more than 'what does the word "w" mean?' – lacks a factual answer. For just as one can distinguish between linguistic and speaker's meaning, between what a word means and what a particular speaker means by it (PON 1, p. 197; PON 2, p. 154), we can distinguish between semantic reference (the name's conventional reference) and speaker's reference (what/who particular speakers have in mind in using it). Thus a referential act may be communicatively successful, yet not denote the right entity or vice versa. (We could distinguish between reference$_{td}$ – a function of communicative success – and reference$_{id}$ – governed by general conventions or standing norms such as N.)

Now let us suppose with Houghton that the famous plays were written by Sir Francis Bacon – the right referent of 'the author of Shakespeare's plays' – and that they had been falsely attributed to an Elizabethan actor by the name of William Shakespeare. It would still be the case that, for the most part, Shakespeare scholars had in mind the author of the plays, whoever he (or she) was, when they used the name 'Shakespeare' in their critical commentaries. It is not a consequence of the Kripkean theory of names that if these plays have been falsely attributed, then centuries of critical comment have to be jettisoned on the grounds that the comments are literally false. Here questions of speaker's reference arise, some of which may call for 'tact and imagination'. In certain cases – for example, in cases of biographical comment on 'Shakespeare' – Rorty is right in saying that we should have a choice between treating them as false remarks about some person or true remarks about another. But none of this shows that there is no fact of the matter about the semantic reference of the name 'William Shakespeare'; nor that that fact is irrelevant in answering these expository questions. What constitutes being the correct semantic referent of the name is being the real owner or bearer of that name.

Finally, Houghton remarks that

> the absence of a general non-trivial account of the reference of names does not mean that the reference has to be, or can be, determined holistically. Whatever the merits of an holistic approach as a general strategy in interpreting a language, it will not produce accuracy of detail. For no interpretation can be accurate that does not take account of linguistic conventions which native speakers themselves recognize, and in the case of some names at least, the historical or causal theorists are right that operative conventions make it possible for speakers' claims about the object named to be largely erroneous. (AM, pp. 168–9)

For instance, on the Baconian hypothesis, it would not be true that 'William Shakespeare wrote Hamlet' or that 'the author of Hamlet was born in Stratford in 1564'.

What of the related Kripkean–Putnamian 'indexical' theory of natural kind terms? There are a number of objections to this, again conceived as a general and substantive account. First, if paradigms for the terms exist, there can be no guarantee that they do exemplify either a natural kind or one and the same natural kind. A Wittgensteinian 'family resemblance' account of the sortal terms of everyday life (tables, chairs) must complement a realist account of those *achieved* in scientific practice (carbon, gold) (cf. RTS, p. 210). But, by the same token, just as Rorty's Davidson-inspired undifferentiated holism – his belief that our utterances are about what most of them are true of – cannot produce *accuracy of detail*, it cannot capture *depth of structure*, as science reveals real underlying essences at work generating and sorting the manifest and messy appearances of the world. Secondly, the application of a natural kind term cannot be determined in general by the nature of the instances to which the term was *originally* applied. For modern science has no access to the internal constitutions of frogs and beech trees that perished centuries ago. If paradigms exist, they must be ours not our ancestors'; and as science progresses paradigms are improved historically (a point that Putnam concedes)[8] until they most closely exemplify our latest theory about the real essence of the natural kind concerned. Thirdly, as noted at page 113 above, natural science typically has an identifying description before and in order for the achievement of p ref. Concepts are prior to the discovery of existents; c ref is prior to p ref. It is a *reductio ad absurdum* of the baptismal theory that if concepts were tied to actual paradigms, it would effectively restrict science to the realm of direct sense-experience. Fourthly, considerations drawn from the practical context of applied science bleed into and infuse the theoretical considerations of pure science. A sample looking and tasting like water on twin earth – say, twater – would probably be accounted water if it were composed of deuterium oxide (heavy water).[9] Finally, a distinction must be made between linguistic and material essentialism.[10] Linguistic essentialism, that there is something that a word *really and intrinsically* means, must be rejected. It is a residue of positivistic or Platonic radical extensionalism. That secretes word – object isomorphism, which breeds linguistic essentialism and material actualism, namely the idea that words denote a constant conjunction of elements, whether empirical or super-empirical (e.g. eidictic, formal). Material essentialism, on the other hand, that each kind of material being has a constituent structure causally responsible for its manifest properties, must be accepted – at least for some scientific domains (e.g. inorganic chemistry). This allows us to reconcile the historical continuity of the use of words like 'copper' and 'poliomyelitis' with discontinuity in (and discovery of) our knowledge of structure.[11]

Both c ref and p ref are involved in the 'search and find' activities of science stressed by two relatively recent writers – Rom Harré [12] and Ian Hacking.[13] Elsewhere, I have detailed a dialectic of scientific discovery, which draws on both descriptivist and essentialist insights (see RTS, chapter 3; and RR, chapter 2.5). We must have putatively identifying descriptions prior to our discovery of underlying structure. But science does uncover the real essences of things. Properly modified, the descriptivist and essentialist theories are better viewed as complementary to each other, stressing different moments of this dialectic, than as rivals.[14] As for Rorty's charge, both descriptivist and essentialist theories of reference can be put to foundationalist use, but neither is necessarily implicated in it. I turn now to Rorty's second motive, his factitious fictionalism. Is there no philosophically significant difference between factual and fictional discourse?

The dialectic of discovery and development in science takes, very schematically, the following characteristic form: Typically, the construction of an explanation for some identified phenomenon will involve the building of a model of a mechanism, which *if* it were to exist and act in the postulated way would account for the phenomenon in question. This is the fictionalist moment in science. 'Let us imagine/suppose/ conjecture/pretend M.' In science, of course, unlike fictional discourse (but in principle like discourse about fiction), the reality of the postulated mechanism or whatever must then be subjected to empirical scrutiny. Once this is done, the explanation must then in principle be itself explained. And so we have a three-phase schema of development in which science identifies a phenomenon (or range of phenomena), constructs explanations for it and empirically tests its explanations, leading to the identification of the generative mechanism at work, which then becomes the phenomenon to be explained, and so on (cf. RR, pp. 19–21). On the ontology of transcendental realism generative mechanisms are analysed out as the causal powers and tendencies of transfactually active things (cf. RTS, chapter 3.3). In this process it is possible that an empirical hypothesis (about the nature of an entity) may become successively a real definition of that entity and as such analytically true, then falsified, as new strata of reality are uncovered, and finally, even eventually fail to refer (as the original entity becomes as theoretically antiquated as caloric or phlogiston).

It is important to note that science employs two criteria for the ascription of reality to a posited object: a perceptual criterion and a causal criterion, neither of which are, of course, satisfied by fictional objects. The causal criterion turns on the capacity of the entity to bring about changes in material things. Notice that a magnetic or gravitational field satisfies this criterion but not a criterion of perceivability. On this criterion to be is not to be perceived, but rather, in the last instance, just to be able to do (cf. RTS, p. 182). If we now, with Roberts,[15] conceive p ref as a theory-led material practice, which involves picking out a figure from a ground, the two criteria are characteristically associated with two different modes of attribution. Associated with the perceptual criterion is a 'DC' mode of attribution, where 'D' stands for a demonstrative and 'C' for a complement, and is exemplified in such statements as 'this grey powder is a sample of gallium'. Associated with the causal criterion is an 'IP' mode of attribution, where 'I' is an indefinite pronoun and 'P' an individuating predicate, exemplified in such statements as 'whatever is the cause of these bubbles is a neutrino'. Generally, the 'D' and 'I' components involve token and the 'C' and 'P' components type reference.[16] Note that in both cases a physical link is established between embodied person and some being – in the first case direct, in the second case mediated. In the 'IP' case 'picking out' a figure from a ground presupposes prior theory about the cause of the bubbles.

How does the fictional moment in science differ from that in literature: 'let us imagine/suppose/conjecture/pretend T'? In the first case, it is not normally spelt out in fiction. It is implicit – and this can be a potential source of confusion, as the furore over *The Satanic Verses* shows. Secondly, it is not normally either tested for truth or meant to be taken as possibly true or as a step in the process of arriving at a corroborated explanation for something. Thirdly, fictional objects are not real on either perceptual or causal criteria, so we have:

1 fictional objects, unlike real objects, do not exist, or more generally are not real; i.e. they do not satisfy the axiom of reality; and
2 fictional objects, in literature, unlike science, are not normally intended to be taken as real.

Directly following on from 1, we have:

3 fictional objects are causally insulated from real objects: they cannot causally interact with them.[17]

This is because causal relations hold only between entities, etc. that are real. As Clark puts it: 'A fictional character cannot kill a real one, although a story about a fictional character might so depress a reader that he committed suicide, or, losing concentration, crashed his car and died. But in those cases what causes the death is not the fictional character, or any activity of that character, but reading the story' (AM, p. 179).

Again, authors create fictional characters, and there is a sense in which they can kill them off, as Conan Doyle once killed off Holmes, but it doesn't follow that they are causally interacting with those characters. Of course, these things cannot be done without *some* causal interactions, but they are interactions with real objects, like pieces of paper, not with fictional ones. *Within* fiction the real and the fictional can interact causally as much as we like [as when an author becomes a character in her novel], but these are only pretended interactions. (AM, p. 179)

Science fiction, like children's fairytales, extend the bounds of our imagination to take in all kinds of physical and conceptual impossibilities, e.g. time travel, species transmutation, etc.; so we can add:

4 what happens in fiction, as opposed to reality, need not be physically or even conceptually possible.

Again, a real object exists and persists whether it is known or appears in a linguistic account, but fictional objects do not – they exist only in virtue of the stories in which they figure. So:

5 real, unlike fictional, objects can exist and act independently of our stories of them.

Other aspects of an adequate ontology and epistemology for science – such as fallibility, transfactuality, counter-phenomenality[18] – possess analogues in fictional discourse.
    Discourse in fiction – (α) – must of course be distinguished from discourse about fiction – (β). In fiction the author creates an imaginary world. This creation is a real event or episode in social reality, which constitutes a terminus for a chain of successful referential acts in (α') the retelling of the story and (β') commentary on it. Both alike are also real events. (α) involves tacitly 'let us pretend T', (α') involves tacitly 'let us follow A's [or the] pretence T' and (β') involves 'on A's pretence T' or 'let us consider A's pretence T'. I have already suggested that Rorty's apparatus is inadequate to deal with (α'). Thus we can refer successfully to Juliet knowing only

that she is a character in a Shakespeare play; so a cluster of descriptions is not necessary. But neither is intention sufficient in (α) or (α'), let alone (β'). Thus I may intend to refer to my character 'Dizzie' and my intention may be effectively thwarted by my prose, or misunderstood by my readers or listeners, i.e. it may not in (textual) fact denote the right character and it may be communicatively unsuccessful. Referring in literature, as in life, is a skilled accomplishment.

Rorty claims, as we have seen, that all we need is the commonsensical notion of 'talking about', where the criterion for what a statement is 'about' is just whatever its utterer 'has in mind'; and he clearly thinks his analysis works equally well for facts and ficts. But, as Clark points out, 'this is simply to ignore the substantial and pervasive differences between the real and the fictitious, a distinction we disregard at our peril. How could it be good to conflate fiction with fact? How could we get along in the world if we did? Our very survival would be threatened by any radical failure to distinguish the two. Indeed, wholesale confusion between the two is taken as a sign of madness' (AM, p. 180).

None of this is, of course, to deny that we can learn from fiction ... But Rorty wants no real-world constraints on discourse. 'Pragmatism ... is the doctrine that there are no constraints on inquiry save conversational ones – no wholesale constraints derived from the nature of the objects, or of the mind, or of language, but only those retail constraints provided by the remarks of our fellow-inquirers' (CP, p. 165). This is tantamount to denying that there is any discernible pattern to scientific enquiry – anything to defictionalize scientific stories. For Rorty: 'There is no method for knowing *when* one has reached the truth, or when one is closer to it than before' (CP, pp. 165–6). But this just returns us to the fundamental paradox of pragmatism. Rorty seems to be claiming an Archimedean position for himself, reoccupying a transcendent standpoint. Moreover, applied to itself, Rorty's pragmatism is self-refuting. This is why Rorty is so careful to claim in his recent writings that he is not arguing with opponents but changing the subject (cf. CIS, chapter 1). But for many, Rorty's subject seems increasingly to be monotonously the same.

Both particular and general existential statements can be falsified in science (and everyday life) – e.g. Vulcan doesn't exist; phlogiston doesn't exist – if either the appropriate demonstrative and/or recognitive criteria are not satisfied (see RTS, p. 178).[19] This leads to a possibility that has been much neglected – what I am going to call *radical negation*. For an entity may be absent from its spatio-temporal [demonstration] region either because it is in some other region – na – or because it does not exist at all – ni – either because it is finite and has perished – ni* – or because it never did exist – ni** (whether it will or may come to exist or not). And the absence of such an entity – let me call this absence n (to cover generically the above cases) – may precisely, *qua* absence, have causal effects on objects in the relevant space–time region, and as such satisfy the causal criterion for ascribing reality to things. Such real absence, including real nonexistence, is radical negation. Think of the missing collar-stud that makes the after-dinner speaker late, the monsoon that doesn't come which makes the crops perish, the inconsolable loss of the bereaved one. We are too apt to miss the importance of the negative in a purely positive account of reality. The tacit assumption is that the negative can always be analysed away in purely positive terms. This is the doctrine of what I shall call ontological monovalence. But it is pure dogma. The world, including the natural world, contains absences, ommissions, liabilities, just as much as presences, commissions and powers.

Not only is the negative underplayed – philosophy's real inheritance from Parmenides; it is also not analysed as a process – of real negation, of subversive or transformative change. This is Plato's legacy to philosophy – the analysis of negation and change in terms of the quite different category of difference. In fact in PMN (chapter 1) Rorty suggests that the problem of the one and the many – the problem of universals – is the one great problem of philosophy. But in the volumes to come we shall see that this problem has always

been circumscribed by that between the one and its negation
or other, which has formed the theme of the dialectical tradition existing, since Plato used dialectic as his mode of access
to the Forms (in the first recognizable fundamentalism),[20] on the
margins of philosophy. In volumes 2 and 3 we shall see how
critical realism, hitherto focusing on the concepts of structure
differentiation and change, has itself to be given a second
edge of analysis, taking in the processual categories of
negation, contradiction, development, becoming, emergence,
finitude and a third level of analysis revolving around the
categories of totality and reflexivity.

NOTES

1   Rorty has three main discussions of it – in TM, PMN (chapter 6)
    and CP (chapter 7).
2   See J. Searle, *Speech Acts*, Cambridge, 1969, p. 77.
3   D. Houghton, 'Rorty's talk-about', AM, p. 162. I am much
    indebted to this excellent article.
4   I borrow a useful expression from R. Boyd, 'Metaphor and
    theory change', *Metaphor and Thought*, ed. A. Ortony, Cam-
    bridge, 1979.
5   Cf. R. Harré, *Varieties of Realism*, Oxford, 1986, p. 107.
6   M. Dummett, *Truth and Other Enigmas*, London, 1968, p. 429.
7   *Naming and Necessity*, Oxford, 1980.
8   H. Putnam, *Realism and Reason*, Cambridge, 1983, chapter 4.
9   Cf. D. H. Mellor, 'Natural kinds', *British Journal for the Philosophy
    of Science* 28 (1977).
10 Cf. *Harré and His Critics*, ed. R. Bhaskar, Oxford, 1990, pp. 4,
    323.
11 On the ontic fallacy, of course, it is easy to confuse linguistic
    and material essentialism, and nominal and real definitions (see
    RTS, p. 211). And this does give some ground for supposing
    that the 'new' theory of reference is, via its radical extensional-
    ism, infected with residues of a sceptical-foundationalist prob-
    lematic.
12 *Varieties of Realism*, Oxford, 1986.
13 *Representing and Intervening*, Cambridge, 1983.
14 Cf. S. Haack, *Philosophy of Logics*, Cambridge, 1978, pp. 64–5.

15 See L. Roberts, in *Synthese*, 1985; cf. Harré, *Varieties of Realism*, especially part 2.
16 Cf. Harré, *Varieties of Realism*, p. 103.
17 Cf. M. Clark, in AM, p. 179.
18 See A. Collier, *An Introduction to Critical Realism*, chapter 1 (forthcoming).
19 For a discussion of the falsification of existential statements in science, see Rom Harré, *Principles of Scientific Thinking*, London, 1970, chapter 3, especially pp. 78–81; and Harré, *Varieties of Realism*, part 2, passim.
20 Or did Plato use fundamentalism to legitimate the practice of dialectic, as Ryle and others have suggested? Or are both true?

8

Rorty's Changing Conceptions of Philosophy

CIS is structured around the distinction between metaphysics and irony (see chapter 4). PMN culminates in the distinction between epistemology and hermeneutics (see chapter 7). In CP one finds a distinction between philosophy as a *Fach* (CP, p. 22; cf. PMN, p. 381) and post-philosophical culture criticism (CP, p. xl; cf. CIS, pp. 32–3). (Is philosophy a or perhaps *the* topic *par excellence* of the latter? In CIS, p. 96 Rorty suggests that metaphysical theory is the topic of ironist theory (but ironist theory comes close to being a contradiction in terms (CIS, p. 120) and should perhaps end in (Derridean) allusion.) But by the end of CIS, philosophy itself has become a private optional obsession (see PDP, p. 292; and CIS, pp. 94, 119 and passim).)[1]

The role of the philosopher is, if shrouded in mystery in CIS, clear enough at the end of PMN and in CP. The philosopher must become a kibitzer (CP, p. 221; PMN, p. 393) whose role-model is that of the all-purpose lawyer (CP, p. 220), whose speciality is argument for the sake not of truth, but of success (so different from the *angst*-ridden obsessive of CIS – with continuing worries about her final vocabularies, nagging doubts about having been born into the wrong tribe). He must become a hermeneut rather than an epistemologist (PMN, chapters 7–8), an 'informed dilettante, the polypragmatic, Socratic intermediary between various discourses', in whose 'salon ... hermetic thinkers are charmed out of their self-enclosed practices' (PMN, p. 317). He is playful, deliberately light-minded, joshing (PDP, p. 293) his contemporaries out of their assumptions. He is a 'strong misreader' (CP, p. 151). Like Derrida, '[he] doesn't want to comprehend Hegel's books; he wants to play with Hegel. He doesn't want to write a book about the nature of language [or indeed about the nature of anything (CIS, p. 21), least of all man (CIS, p. 4 and passim; CP, pp. 206–8)];[2] he wants to play with all the texts which other people have thought they were writing about language' (CP, p. 96; cf. CIS, chapter 6). He 'feels free to comment on anything at all. He is the prefiguration of the all-purpose intellectual of a post-Philosophical culture, the philosopher who has abandoned pretensions to Philosophy [i.e. renounced Philosophy as a *Fach* (CP, p. 201)]. He passes rapidly from Hemingway to Proust to Hitler to Marx to Foucault to the present situation in south-east Asia to Gandhi to Sophocles. He is a name- dropper [cf. also CP, pp. 65, 92], who uses names such as these to refer to sets of descriptions, symbol-systems, ways of seeing. His speciality is seeing similarities and differences between great big pictures, between attempts to see how things hang together' (CP, p. xl). He is the redescriber who redescribes redescriptions, who totalizes (or deconstructs) totalities, who refuses to think of his meta-narrative as anything more than just another poem. But he is 'doomed to become outdated' (redescribed, out-totalized). 'For nobody is so passé as the intellectual czar of the previous generation – the man who redescribed all those old descriptions, which, thanks in part to his redescription of them, nobody now wants to hear anything about' (CP, pp. xl–xli).

He is a 'bookish intellectual' (CP, xxxviii), who 'denies the possibility of going beyond the Sellarsian notion of "seeing how things hang together"[3] – which means 'seeing how all the various vocabularies of all the various cultures and epochs hang together' (ibid.). His hero is Dewey, whose 'chief enemy was the notion of Truth and accuracy of representation' (CP, p. 86) and who 'thought that if he could only break down this notion ... we would be receptive to notions like Derrida's –

that language is not a device for representing reality, but a reality in which we live and move' (CP, p. 87). He denies that it is possible 'to step outside our skins – the traditions, linguistic and other, within which we do our thinking and self-criticism – and compare ourselves with something absolute' (CP, p. xix); that there is something 'deep down beneath all the texts ... which is not just one more text but that to which various texts are trying to be "adequate"' (ibid.).

Rorty is a nominalist about philosophy – 'philosophy ... is just whatever us philosopher professors do' (CP, p. 220) – '[it] is not the name of a natural kind' (CP, p. 226). But PMN has all the characteristics of a 'meta-narrative' in Lyotard's sense.[4] And a formal dilemma can be applied to disciplinary nominalism. For either there are *real differences* between the activities of philosophers and stand-up comedians, in virtue of which the predicate 'philosophical' is applicable to the former, but not (as such) to the latter; or else there are no grounds for *consistently* using the term 'philosopher' to designate one rather than another group of people. At any rate, there is no doubt that Rorty does think that Philosophy as hitherto practised should make way for a new post-Philosophical culture. Should it cease altogether? Rorty is equivocal on this, seeing that the new culture may be parasitic on the old. A central feature of the new culture is the replacement of science by literature in terms of its centrality and in particular its centrality to philosophy's concerns. We have already noted (in chapter 1) the problems this raises should philosophy be central or important to science.

The theme of a post-Philosophical culture is an old one in Rorty. In LT (pp. 33ff) he considers six 'possibilities for the future of philosophy, after the dissolution of the traditional problems' (LT, p. 34). These are the ways of Husserlian phenomenology, Heidegger, Waismann, Wittgenstein, Austinian and Strawsonian linguistic philosophy. It is clear that Rorty is happiest with the third.

Philosophers could then turn towards creating Ideal Languages, but the criterion for being 'Ideal' would no longer be

the dissolution of philosophical problems, but rather the creation of new, interesting and fruitful ways of thinking about
things in general. This would amount to a return to the great
tradition of philosophy as system-building – the only difference
being that the systems built would no longer be considered
descriptions of the nature of things, but rather *proposals* about
how to talk. By such a move, the 'creative' and 'constructive'
function of philosophy could be retained. Philosophers would
be, as they are traditionally supposed to be, men who gave one
a *Weltanschauung* – in Sellars' phrase, a way of understanding
how things in the broadest possible sense of the term hang
together in the broadest possible sense of the term. (LT, p. 34)

By the time of PMN, Rorty has turned against constructive
system-building in favour of peripheral, reactive and pragmatic philosophers who, while they kibitz about practically everything, are precisely 'sceptical about systematic philosophy
[and] the whole project of universal commensuration' (PMN,
p. 368). 'In our time, Dewey, Wittgenstein and Heidegger are
the great edifying, peripheral thinkers. All three make it as
difficult as possible to take their thought as expressing views
on traditional philosophical problems, or as making constructive proposals for philosophy as a cooperative and progressive
discipline' (ibid.). This tendency is taken to the limit in the
purely private allusions of Derrida apotheosized in CIS
(chapter 6). This is more the Nietzschean overcoming
of philosophy, than the Kantian–Hegelian completion, the
Humean–positivist dissolution, the early Marxian realization
or the Wittgensteinian linguistic philosophic transformation of
it. He sees, however, that philosophy has a continuing underlabouring (or apologetic) role in relation to politics – for liberal
democracy.

This study has been primarily critical of Rorty. But it shares
with Rorty a starting point he attributes to his teachers of
philosophy: 'that a "philosophical problem" was a product of
the unconscious adoption of assumptions built into the vocabulary in which the problem was stated – assumptions which
were to be questioned before the problem itself was taken

seriously' (PMN, p. xiii). I would argue too that certain pervasive assumptions about the nature of knowledge, the world and
their relations underpin the philosophical tradition and inform
much contemporary culture, including the practice of social
science. In their standard forms, these assumptions are that
knowledge is or must be incorrigible and permanent, that the
world is essentially unstructured, undifferentiated and unchanging, and that the relationship between knowledge and
the world is one of isomorphism or even identity, i.e. such
that knowledge replicates, mirrors and reflects the world,
typically in what I have called the 'ontic fallacy'. It is this
image that Rorty captures and demolishes so well, especially
in PMN. But he does not see that these assumptions are
undergirded by what I have called the 'epistemic fallacy', the
definition of being in terms of knowledge. Moreover, underlying these mistakes are certain prevalent misconceptions about
both the nature of the world – actualism – and the nature of
human beings in society – atomism.[5] It is Rorty's failure to
thematize philosophical ontology and sociology and his consequent subscription to the epistemic fallacy that leads to the
replication of classical problems as (displaced or undisplaced)
aporiai in his work. Thus the problem of induction becomes
the problem of how poetic or intellectual change, or even
criticism, is possible (see chapter 6 above). The Kantian resolution of the antinomy between free will and determinism is
replicated in the aporiai in which his philosophy of action is
mired (see chapter 3 above).

Rorty uses certain standard gambits again and again to
'overcome the problematic'. We noticed in chapter 1 his 'dis-
junctivitis' – his continual posing of dichotomies between, on
the one hand, a hard fundamentalist demand usually steeped
in actualist folklore and, on the other, a soft deflationary
option, usually with voluntaristic overtones or leanings. Rorty
is a most undialectical thinker. Why cannot language be both
a device for representing reality and a reality in which we live
and move (*contra* CP, p. 87). Why cannot knowledge have
vertical and horizontal components, reveal depth and change?
Why cannot science show a non-algorithmic pattern?

A second gambit Rorty uses is his heavy steamroller – levelling down distinctions, softening and blurring these until a fuzzy borderline is all. But the existence of fuzzy borders does not gainsay clear distinctions between the necessary and contingent, the (relatively) *a priori* and the (relatively) empirical, or between (conceptual) scheme and (datal) content. Again Rorty, following Davidson, settles for an unstratified, undifferentiated holism, which denies the existence of any structurally significant or detailed falsity. Even Davidson is forced to remark that there are two respects in which interpretaters can differ over whether an utterance is true; viz. (1) how things are in the world they share, and (2) what the utterance means[6] – which correspond exactly to content and scheme!

A third gambit is his insider–outsider flip. This characteristically shows itself in an ethnocentricism about politics and a transcendentism about philosophy. Closely related to the former too is his emotivism, and his subscription to what I called in chapter 2 the anti-naturalistic fallacy.

Fourth, there is his unconscious displacement of the traditional philosophical problematic – his proto-positivism about political facts and his aloneness in philosophical self-invention. But even before CIS he accepted the dichotomy of a neutral, but not very helpful, observation language – the epitome of normal discourse – shared between unique self-individuating individuals, seeking their individuation in the zone of the abnormal. So we come to his final gambit – the single fault-line that runs throughout his work – between the abnormal new and the normal old. At the same time his referential fictionalism allows him to deny both that he is arguing self-refutingly and that he is not arguing to the point. He is changing the subject, breaking new ground, dynamiting the old.

The question that is obviously raised by this critique of Rorty is: why Rorty? I suggest that Rorty provides an ideology for a leisured elite – intellectual yuppies – neither racked by pain nor immersed in toil – whose lives may be devoted to the practice of aesthetic enhancement, and in particular to generating self, other and genealogical descriptions. Their careers are a succession of poems, all marginally different; and a succession of paradigm shifts, for which no overarching or commensurating criteria can be given. They resemble Novalis and the Romantics, whom Hegel criticized so memorably in his discussion of the 'beautiful soul'. They are to be found especially in the 'soft' disciplines – the social sciences and humanities – where experimental closures are not possible and where there appear to be no criteria for rational criticism and change (cf. PON, chapter 4). Rorty may be considered as the ideologue of unschematized categories and concepts for a leisured elite, in conditions of plenty. But he counts 'among the philosophers' (cf. CS, p. 15) – having redescribed the impress of the problematic in terms which are more than marginally his own.

NOTES

1   Thus: 'The metaphysician's association of theory with social hope and of literature with private perfection is, in an ironist liberal culture, reversed. Within a liberal metaphysical culture the disciplines which were charged with penetrating behind the many private appearances to the one general common reality – theology, science, philosophy – were the ones which were expected to bind human beings together, and thus to help eliminate cruelty. Within an ironist culture, by contrast, it is the disciplines which specialize in thick description of the private and idiosyncratic which are assigned this job. In particular, novels and ethnographies which sensitise us to the pain of those who do not speak our language must do the job which demonstrations of a common human nature were supposed to do ... Conversely, within our increasingly ironist culture, philosophy has become more important for the pursuit of private perfection rather than for any social task' (CIS, p. 94).
2   In the later Rorty, human nature becomes *the* subject of philosophy (see e.g. PDP, p. 264).
3   See W. Sellars, *Science, Perception and Reality*, London, 1963, p. 1.
4   *The Post-modern Condition*, Manchester, 1984 (cf. HLP).

5   Cf. C. Taylor, 'Overcoming epistemology', *After Philosophy*, ed. K. Beynes, J. Bohman and T. McCarthy, Cambridge, Mass., 1987.

6   Donald Davidson, 'A coherence theory of truth and knowlege', in *Truth and Interpretation: Perspectives on the Philosophy of Donald Davidson*, ed. E. LePore, Oxford, 1986, p. 309.

Section Two

For Critical Realism

9

Critical Realism in Context

It is my aim in this chapter to sketch the main lines of critical
realism, and to indicate how it would deal with critical theory,
as represented by Habermas, and postmodernism. I take
Rorty as emblematic of postmodernism.

Critical theory antedates both critical realism and postmodernism. But although postmodernism is sometimes said not to
exist as a phenomenon, and it is sometimes given as specific a
birth-date as the dynamiting, at 3.32 p.m. on 15 July 1972, of
the (Le Corbusier-based) Pruitt-Igoe housing development in
St Louis, it seems fair to see it emerging as a distinct cultural
tendency at about the same time as critical realism. That is to
say, both can be seen as emerging in the material context,
historical conjuncture, between 1968 and 1976, defined by:

1   the end of the long post-war boom;
2   the defeat of the left in a protracted period of international
    social and especially class struggles, only partially offset by
    the defeat of US imperialism in Vietnam;
3   the birth or renewal of the new social movements – stu-
    dent, feminist, green, peace, etc.;
4   a partial transition from Fordism to a new, more flexible
    regime of accumulation;
5   a new round of what David Harvey has called 'space–time
    compression',[1] exemplified by the first man on the moon

walk in 1969, the ubiquity of jet travel and new computer-based information technologies;

6   the crisis and demise of the formerly hegemonic positivist account of science and knowledge.

Critical realism and Rorty's work represent two responses to the crisis of positivism. (Habermas represents another.) This has two main axes. In the first place a crisis of representation, induced by the attacks of Popperians, Kuhnians and Wittgensteinians on positivism's monistic theory of scientific development. These attacks I wove into my account of the transitive or epistemological dimension of the philosophy of science. Secondly, a crisis of legitimacy, induced by the attacks from Scriven, Hesse and Harré on the lack of *sufficiency* of Humean and Hempelian criteria in positivism's deductivist theory of scientific structure. I generalized these attacks and argued that Humean and Hempelian criteria were not *necessary* either for causal laws, etc. (which had to be seen as the transfactually efficacious tendencies of structures and generative mechanisms irreducible to patterns of events and the operations of human beings alike) in my account of the intransitive or ontological dimension of the philosophy of science.

Rom Harré had employed the rhetoric of Copernicanism to describe his switch in focus from deductive structure to animating model.[2] I took over the rhetoric but used it to connote two other ideas:

1   the switch, within ontology, from events to mechanisms (the exoteric meaning);
2   the switch, within philosophy, from epistemology to ontology (the esoteric meaning).

The key moment here was the isolation of the epistemic fallacy – the definition or analysis of being in terms of knowledge; and more generally the anthropomorphic fallacy, including the linguistic fallacy. The ideological point of the epistemic fallacy was the complementary ontic fallacy – the ontologization, naturalization or eternalization of knowledge (e.g. through its compulsive determination by being). The ontic fallacy is noticed by Rorty in *Philosophy and the Mirror of Nature*; he however remains wedded to the epistemic fallacy and committed to the Humean–Hempelian view of science which presupposes it.

The development of transcendental or critical realism presupposes a philosophical method imbued with Aristotelian, Baconian, Lockean, Leibnizian, Kantian, Hegelian and Marxian moments. And it consists in an account of science developed in three main dimensions: intransitive, transitive and metacritical.

Critical realism is not just a scientifically oriented realism but a scientific realism, i.e. a philosophy *for*, not just *of* science. However, it is not the only scientific realism and in particular it is not a scientistic realism, i.e. a realism which attributes overwhelming evaluative and/or historically explanatory pre-eminence to the social institutions of science. Critical realism is the core of a research programme rather than an exhaustive account of the sciences. Its premises are historical, and like all knowledge it is essentially transformable and open to development. However, I think that critical realism is uniquely consistent with the historical emergence, substantive content and practical presuppositions of the fundamental explanatory sciences as we know them today.[3] Moreover, transferred to the context of the human sciences, critical realism is immediately liberating. For such sciences deal in necessarily open systems, where positivism's instrumentalist-predictive-manipulative approach to phenomena is completely out of place.

I turn now to the development of critical naturalism in the social sciences. Critical naturalism or realism transcends three crude polarities:

1 It affirms a relational conception of the subject-matter of the human sciences in opposition to individualism and collectivism.

2 Its transformational model of social activity avoids the errors of reification and voluntarism alike.
3 Its qualified critical naturalism is opposed to both positivistic hyper-naturalism and hermeneutical total anti-naturalism.

On analysis, ontological, epistemological, relational and critical differences emerge between the natural and the human sciences. Examination of the critical difference (see Appendix 1) allows us to illustrate the passage from fact to value, theory to practice. Associated with this is a defintion of emancipation and a richer conception of human freedom than the existing traditions have been able to sustain.

Why is critical realism critical? First, because it is transcendental; secondly, because it situates a contingently critical hermeneutics (see PON 1 p. 177; PON 2, p. 138); and thirdly, because it exhibits a mechanism of ideology-critique, which can be generalized to the critique of social systems on grounds of their incapacity to allow the fulfilment of other human needs, wants and interests (besides truth) (see SR, chapter 2.5–7).[4]

I now want briefly to critically situate Habermas from the standpoint of critical realism. First, he remains ensnared in the antinomy of transcendental pragmatism: nature cannot both pre-exist and be constituted by society (see RR, p. 141). Secondly, he does not break from the epistemic fallacy. He tacitly inherits a positivist ontology and an instrumentalist-manipulative conception of the interest informing the natural sciences and the sphere of labour as distinct from communicative interaction and from discourse (which is hermetically sealed off from action, leading *inter alia* to an only weakly elaborated 'evidential dimension'). Finally, as Habermas's emancipatory interest is derivative from his communicative interest, his system readily takes on a dualistic, overly anti-naturalist hue in which the extra-communicative or extra-discursive constraints on communicative action are marginalized – only to reappear later in the *Theory of Communicative Action* where they are set at loggerheads with the latter in the guise of the colonization of the noumenal lifeworld by the phenomenal reified systems of the economy and polity coordinated by the media of money and power (see RR, p. 189).

I return now to Rorty. First, he remains wedded to a positivist account of natural science. He has no theory of justification and erects a Nietzschean superstructure (as a super-idealist 'epistmology') in the guise of an undifferentiated 'linguistified' monism on a Humean–Hempelian ontological base. His contrast between epistemology and hermeneutics is drawn without regard for the differences between the natural and the human sciences (he is a hyper-naturalist). Secondly, the problematic of PMN replicates the Kantian resolution to the third antinomy: we are determined as material bodies, but free as discursive (speaking and writing) subjects. Rorty's actualism (like Kant's) makes human agency impossible. Finally, there is an antinomy within the antinomy as Rorty in his later work distinguishes private perfection (irony) from public pragmatism (morality). A late-coming ideologue of the Cold War, he defines morality as 'we-intentions', where 'we' are the 'leisured, educated policy-makers of the North Atlantic bourgeoisie'.

What is the relationship between Marxism and critical realism? In the first place, radical social change presupposes depth realism; Marx's work at its best illustrates critical realism; and critical realism is the absent methodological fulcrum of Marx's work (as we shall see in Appendix 2) (cf. RR, chapter 7). Secondly, the transitive dimension in critical realism is congruent with a Marxist theory of society and is influenced by it. Thirdly, critical realism employs many Marxian analogues in the analysis and critique of positivism and idealist epistemologies generally – e.g. the fetishism of the fact form intrinsic to normal science – but the validity of the concept in the new domain is logically independent of its validity in the source domain from which it was drawn (cf. e.g. the concept of 'force' in physics). Finally, there is an elective affinity between critical realism and historical materialism, in that *inter alia* critical realism is a heterocosmic instance of the emancipatory transformation socialism aspires to achieve.

Critical realism is equally opposed to the new realism of the labour right and the new idealism of the academy. But it is also opposed to dogmatic fundamentalism (see RR, p. 191). In place of these we need to ask, to what extent are enduring structures being reproduced in novel forms and to what extent are they being transformed? 'Reality' must be 'reclaimed' in two senses. First, the concept must be reclaimed from philosophical ideologies which have usurped or denied it – reclamation in the sense of lost property. Second, reality itself must be rescued from the effects of those ideologies that have, like stagnant and muddy water, covered it up – reclamation in the sense of land reclamation.[5] What should be done with reality once it is reclaimed? It should, I suggest, be used, nurtured and valued in an ecologically sustainable and humane way for human emancipation, happiness and flourishing.

NOTES

1 *The Condition of Postmodernity*, Oxford, 1989, especially part III.
2 See *The Principles of Scientific Thinking*, London, 1970.
3 See RR, chapter 9; and PON 2, 'Postscript'.
4 Cf. Jeffrey Isaac, 'Realism and Reality: Some Realistic Reconsiderations', *Journal for the Theory of Social Behaviour*, 20(1), (1990) and William Outhwaite, 'Realism, Naturalism and Social Behaviour', *Journal for the Theory of Social Behaviour* 20(4), (1990).
5 See William Outhwaite, 'Lost and found', *Times Higher Educational Supplement*, 15 September 1989, p. 20.

Appendix 1

Social Theory and Moral Philosophy

It is my overall argument that the fact–value and theory–practice distinctions, as developed and presented in contemporary ethics and orthodox philosophy of social science, are completely untenable. While facts and theories are influenced by our values and practices, it is also possible rationally to derive value and practical judgements from deep explanatory social theories. The textbook doctrine that fact and value, theory and practice belong to different realms creates an artificial barrier between sociology and ethics. It is my contention that, on the contrary, social theory just is moral philosophy, but as science.

I have three main aims in this appendix. My primary aim is to show what must be the case for an emancipatory social science to be possible. Emancipation is not to be confused with the amelioration of states of affairs. Nor does it involve the absence of determination. It consists in the transformation or replacement of unneeded, unwanted and oppressive sources of determination, or structures, by needed, wanted and empowering ones. My conception of emancipation is grounded in agents' empirically manifest wants and identifiable needs. But to the extent that some social transformation

This paper develops the argument of PON, chapter 2; SR, chapters 2 and 3; and RR, chapter 6 and passim.

is to be rationally emancipatory it depends not only or especially on a science of behaviour, but on a science – a depth science – of the structures generating, determining or providing the sources of behaviour. It is my intention to defend the scientificity, and elucidate the general form, of such depth-enquiries in the human sciences. This will necessitate an excursus into the philosophy of science, and more particularly social science, in the earlier part of my essay. My secondary aim is to resolve the traditional antinomies between fact and value and theory and practice; that is, to transcend the oppositions between (in a broad sense) positivism and moralism, scientism and criticism, science and critique, scientific explanation and human emancipation. My argument is that social science is non-neutral in a double sense – in that it both (a) consists in a practical intervention in social life and (b) logically entails values. It is the conative role of belief-informed and realizable wants and the explanatory power of (agents') theories which play the crucial role in these transitions.

My third and final aim is to provide a critique of 'Hume's law'. The generally accepted, and in my opinion essentially correct, interpretation of Hume is that he enunciated what has become – at least since the publication of Moore's *Principia Ethica* – an article of faith for the entire analytical tradition, namely that the transition from 'is' to 'ought', factual to value statements, indicatives to imperatives, is, although frequently made (and perhaps even, like eduction, psychologically necessary), logically inadmissible. In contrast, I want to argue that provided only certain minimal conditions are satisfied, it is not only acceptable, but logically mandatory.

The critical realist account of science (which I first elaborated in *A Realist Theory of Science*[1] and has subsequently been developed by myself and others) can only be briefly summarized here. It has three main aspects. First, in *ontology*, it involves the transcendental refutation of the empiricist ontology informing the hitherto dominant accounts of science, and its replacement by a more complex ontology, on which the world appears as structured, differentiated and changing.

From the standpoint of the philosophy of social science, the most important point to note here is that the absence of closed systems (and the impossibility of crucial experiments) means that criteria for the rational assessment of theories cannot be predictive and so must be exclusively explanatory. Secondly, in *epistemology*, it involves the elaboration of a rational account of scientific activity, which is conceived as engaged in the continual process of the empirically controlled retroduction of explanatory structures from the manifest phenomena which are produced by them. Thirdly, in what I have called the *metacritical dimension*, it consists in an examination of the metaphysical and social bases of accounts of science and the elaboration of a new conception of philosophy, on which it is conceived as incorporating aspects of Aristotelian dialectic, Lockean underlabouring, Leibnizian conceptual analysis, Kantian transcendental argumentation, Hegelian dialectical phenomenology, Marxian critique of the speculative illusion and Baconian-Bachelardian value commitment.

Applied to the domain of the social sciences, this perspective – of transcendental realism – enables a *critical naturalism*, based on an independent analysis of what must be the case for intentional action to be possible. This involves in the first place a critique of individualist and collectivist conceptions of the subject-matter of social science in favour of a relationist conception, on which its subject-matter is conceived as, paradigmatically, the enduring relationships between individuals and groups and their artefacts and nature and functions of them – relationships such as those between parents and children, employer and employees, employees and the unemployed, and so on. Secondly, it necessitates articulation of the duality of social structure and human agency or praxis,[2] namely, that social structures are a necessary condition for human agency (as its means and media) but that they exist and persist only in virtue of human agency – the human agency which reproduces or transforms them. This entails what I have called the transformational model of social activity. (See figures 1 and 2.) This model has a number of consequences. First, actors' accounts are limited by unintended

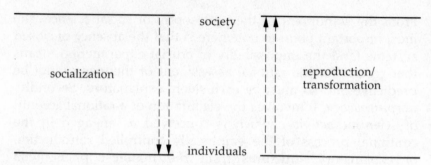

Figure 1 The transformational model of social activity

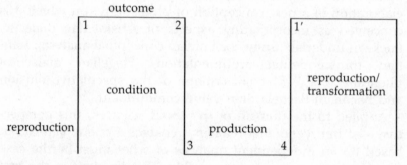

Figure 2 Structure and praxis
Note: 1,1' = unintended consequences; 2 = unacknowledged conditions;
      3 = unconscious motivations; 4 = tacit skills.

consequences, unacknowledged conditions, unconscious motivation and tacit skills. Figures 2 and 4 show the feedback of
consequences on the conditions of actions. It follows from the
limitations on actors' knowledge that social science has a
possible cognitive role to play for human agents. And from
this there follows a critique of the doctrine of interpretive
fundamentalism: there is no incorrigible foundational base of
social scientific knowledge in actors' accounts. The recursive
and non-teleological character of society also follows from the
transformational model of social activity. As an object of
enquiry, society is nothing other than the ensemble of the
unmotivated conditions for our substantive motivated produc-

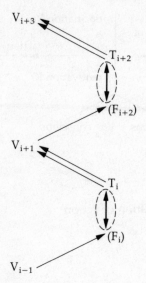

Figure 3 Fact/value helix
Note: V, T, (F) stand for values, theories and sets of facts respectively.

Table 1

$V \nrightarrow F$	scientism
$F \nrightarrow V$	positivism (and displacements)
$T \nrightarrow P$	irrationalism
$T \Rightarrow P$	theoreticism (idealism) ($\rightarrow P \nrightarrow T$)

Note: F stands for facts and theories.

tions. As such it must be seen as a causally and taxonomically irreducible mode of matter – with the natural and social worlds conceived as in dynamic interrelationship. The transformational model of social activity also implies a series of ontological, relational, epistemological and critical limits on naturalism. I discussed the first three kinds of limits in *The Possibility of Naturalism*,[3] and defend my account of them in a postscript to the second edition. It is the fourth kind of limit that I am concerned with here, as I come to the main point of

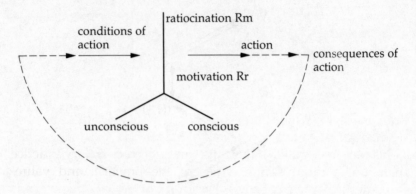

Figure 4   The stratification of action

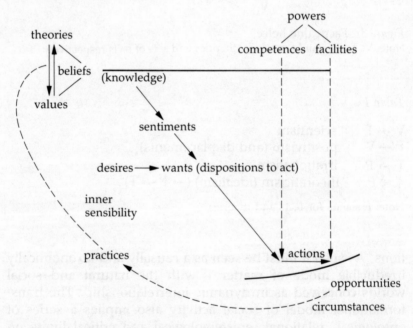

Figure 5   The five bases of action and practices, values and theories

my essay: a critique of the doctrine of the value-neutrality of social science.

My contention is that while theoretical and factual considerations both causally presage and logically entail practical and evaluative ones, practical and evaluative considerations causally predispose but do not entail theoretical and factual ones. So that although there is mutual interdependence, there is not mutual entailment, which makes the fact/value helix displayed in Figure 3 (and its undisplayed theory/practice analogue) a rational one. I accept the practical and value-dependent character of social enquiry, but my main concern is to show how explanatory theories entail values and practices. And my core argument turns on the fact that the subject-matter of the social sciences includes both social objects and beliefs about those objects; and that any disjuncture or mismatch between them may enter into social explanation; so that if we can *explain* the (perhaps contingent) *necessity* for false (illusory) consciousness, then we may pass immediately to a negative evaluation of the source(s) of false consciousness; and to a positive evaluation on action rationally directed at removing it, in the way indicated in Inference Scheme 1.

I now turn more generally to Hume's Law and its criticism. Hume's Law, that one cannot derive an 'ought' from an 'is', is historically closely associated with the scientistic principle, which I shall label (1), viz. that social scientific propositions are logically independent of value positions. Hume's Law may then be stated as (2): value positions are logically independent of social scientific positions. And (1) and (2) may be represented as:

(1) $V \nrightarrow F$
(2) $F \nrightarrow V$

It is important to keep the two distinct, for nowadays (1), very much out of vogue in postmodernist thought, is quite often rejected, while (2) is still largely held sacrosanct. However, it will be seen that without a rejection of (2) as well, rejection of (1) injects a moment of arbitrariness into the social scientific

Inference Schemes

I.S.I. (i) $T > P$. (ii) $T \exp 1(P) \rightarrow$ (iii) $-V(S \rightarrow I(P)) \rightarrow$
  (iv) $V\phi_{-s}$

Note: (i) = critical condition;
   (ii) = explanatory condition;

Further (e.g. categorial) conditions may be specified.

I.S.2 $T > P$. $T \exp X(P) \rightarrow -V(S \rightarrow X(P)) \rightarrow V\phi_{-s}$

I.S.3 $T \exp$. $I-H$. $-V(I-H) \rightarrow -V(S \rightarrow I-H) \rightarrow V\phi_{-s}$

I.S.4 $T > P$.$T \exp.I-H$. $T \exp.(I-H \rightarrow I(P)) \rightarrow$
   $-V(S \rightarrow I-H) \rightarrow \phi V_{-s}$

(5) $s \rightarrow p$. $sp \rightarrow \psi$

(6) $S \rightarrow (s \rightarrow p$. $sp \rightarrow \psi) \rightarrow S'$

(7) $E \rightarrow A$. $EA \rightarrow P$

(8) $R \rightarrow (E \rightarrow A$. $EA \rightarrow P) \rightarrow R'$

I.S.9 $T > P$. $T \exp -S_c(I(P)) \rightarrow -V(S \rightarrow -S_c(I(P))) \rightarrow$
   $V\phi_{-s}$

I.S.10 $T > P$. $T \exp -S_o(I(P)) \rightarrow -V(S \rightarrow -S_o(I(P)))$
   $\rightarrow V\phi_{-s}$

Conditions of the Posssibility of Emancipatory Practices:
1. causality of reasons
2. immanence of values
3. internality of critique
4. coincidence of subjective needs and objective
   possibilities
5. knowable emergence

process. I want to argue against (1) and (3), irrationalism, that, *pace* Hume, it is irrational to prefer the destruction of the world to that of my little finger (i.e. against moral contingentism, or scepticism – a direct analogue of the problem of induction); and against (2) and (4), theoreticism, entailing moral actualism which makes akrasia impossible. More generally, I want to combat the dismissal of the descriptive or ontological grounds in virtue of which some belief or action is commended or recommended in favour of the prescriptive, imperatival or practical component which could be called the *anti-naturalistic fallacy* in axiology, whether this is given a communitarian or individualist declension, and whether it takes a Nietzschean or Weberian, an emotivist or decisionist form.

(1) has been criticized from the standpoint of the subjectivity of (a) the subject and (b) the object, as well as (leading on from (b)) (c) the relationship between the two. (a) is concerned with the value-bias of social science, (b) with the value-impregnation of its subject-matter, and (c) with that of any adequate description of it.

At (a) it has been argued that the social values of the scientist or scientific community determine or influence (1) the selection of problems, (2) the conclusions, and even (3) the standards of enquiry (for example, by Weber, Myrdal and Mannheim, respectively). (1), often treated as uncontroversial, fails to distinguish between the pure and applied sciences, whether social or natural. In pure science choice of the object of study is governed by the search for explanatory mechanisms, while in applied science it may be motivated by the industrial, technological, medical, military, financial or more generally socio-cultural significance of the properties, whether natural or social. (2) is altogether more powerful. But if the distortion due to the value-bound-upness of the subject in or by the object is unconscious then Myrdal's influential solution for the scientist to state at the outset his value position will not work – for it presupposes that she can have the sort of knowledge about herself which she cannot have *ex hypothesi* about society. Moreover, one cannot say in general whether avowals will be more or less misleading. (3) posits a relativity of standards of enquiry, and is just a special case of the general problem of relativism. I take the objective here to be to avoid both epistemic absolutism and judgemental irrationalism. I would like to do so by accepting epistemic relativism, which asserts that all beliefs are socially produced, so all knowledge is transient, and neither truth-values nor criteria of rationality exist outside historical time; but rejecting judgemental relativism, which claims that there are no good grounds for preferring one to another set of beliefs. Epistemic relativism, unlike judgemental relativism, is not self-refuting; nor is it gainsaid by the mere facts of intersubjective communication, translation and interpretation.[4]

Arguments of type (b) turn on the constitution of the subject-matter of social science by objects of value. The norm of descriptive adequacy, which depends upon but may outstrip (in a metacritique) hermeneutic adequacy, entails the contingent necessity for value-laden descriptions. Consider Isaiah Berlin's famous example of what happened in Germany under Nazi rule. The statement that 'millions of people were massacred' is not only more evaluative, but more precise and accurate than the increasingly anaemic and unsatisfactory statements that 'millions of people were killed', 'millions of people died' and 'the country was depopulated'. In short, not to call a spade a spade in any human society is to misdescribe it. Dogma (1), then, must be rejected on the grounds that it ignores the subject's interest in the object, and the fact that the nature of the object is such that criteria for descriptive (and more generally explanatory) adequacy entail the possibility of irreducibly evaluative descriptions. But without a rejection of (2) a potential element of arbitrariness (leading to the possibility of a radical conventionalism) may enter into the scientific process. For why should we not generate in the light of our special interests whatever facts we please? So let us turn to (2). Before offering my own account of the matter, I want to discuss three recent attempts to break down the fact/value distinction along the axis denied in (2).

Taylor's argument, which may be represented as (3) $T \leftrightarrow F \rightarrow V$, shows clearly how theories do, in fact, secrete values. Unfortunately, however, by failing to specify any criterion for choosing between theories, he leaves himself open to the interpretation that one should choose the theory that most satisfies our conception of what 'fulfils human needs, wants and purposes', thus merely displacing rather than transcending the fact/value dichotomy. The structure of Searle's argument, which may be represented as (4) I.F. $\rightarrow V$, depends on the critical 'is' statement describing institutional facts. But

---

Scientism: $V \nrightarrow F$

Hume's Law: $F \nrightarrow V$

Taylor's argument: $T \leftrightarrow F \rightarrow V$

Searle's argument: $I.F. \rightarrow V$

Prior's argument: $F.F. \rightarrow V$

My argument:
(6) $T > P. \; T \exp I(P) \rightarrow - V(S \rightarrow I(P)) \rightarrow V\phi_{-s}$

---

location within an institution, such as promising, does not warrant a normative or moral commitment to the institution – otherwise it would be impossible to be a socialist within a capitalist society or a liberal within a totalitarian one. To derive a morally unrevocable (CP) 'ought' from an 'is', one has to move from premises that are constitutive of purely factual discourse, that are transcendentally necessary. Arguments by A. N. Prior, Philippa Foot and others, which may be represented as (5) $F.F. \rightarrow V$, depend on the critical 'is' statement describing functional facts, such that if 'X' is such and such it is a good watch, knife, farmer, sea captain or whatever, are subject to a similar objection. For one may object to what it is, in any determinate society, to be a good farmer – does this entail battery or hothouse techniques of production? – or the uses to which, e.g., knives are typically put. Anscombe's generalization of this point in the notion of flourishing such that from 'X is flourishing' we can logically deduce 'X is good' similarly begs the question whether it is good that X, a member or the whole of a particular species, flourishes, whatever empirically flourishing may be agreed to consist in, e.g. if this is at the expense of other members or species.

My argument, it is important to note, does not permit a simple inference from facts to values. It turns, rather, on the capacity of a theory to explain false consciousness. If one is in possession of a theory that explains why false consciousness is necessary, then one can pass immediately, without the addition of any extraneous value judgement, to a negative evaluation on the object that makes such consciousness necessary and to a positive evaluation on action rationally directed at removing it. It is important to stress that the point about my core argument is not only that it formally refutes Hume's Law, and not just that it *per se* delineates the structure of motivating argument for rational radical political or therapeutic action, but rather that it may be generalized from the critique of credibly false consciousness to take in the critique of all those other seemingly necessary ills – amounting to the non-fulfilment of human needs, wants, potentialities, interests and aspirations – which together may constitute grounds for being a radical (that is committed to deliberate transformation of society in a fundamental manner). But is there a sense in which Inference Scheme 1 is transcendentally necessary? Yes – there can be no action without beliefs and no beliefs save by work on or with other beliefs, so judgements of falsity, inconsistency, etc. are inescapable. Moreover, it is only if an agent can explain a belief that she can set out rationally to change it, in the case where the belief proves unsusceptible to direct criticism. If beliefs are not to be given a totally voluntaristic explanation – if they are at all recalcitrant (like other social objects – including the rest of the social structure, as is implied by their internality to it) – and/or if a sociology of knowledge is to be possible and/or necessary (and one is already implicit in lay practice), then the form of explanation schematized in Inference Scheme 1 is a condition of every rational practice. The possibility of coming to say: 'now this is why you (I/she) erroneously believe(d) such and such' is a presupposition of every rational discourse or authentic act of self-reflection at all. It is important to stress here that it is not so much the existence of false consciousness *per se* but the existence of false grounds for consciousness – that is, of a real/assumed grounds for beliefs distinction – that renders the inference scheme transcendentally necessary. It is the existence of deep necessary falsity that is at issue here.

Figure 3 indicates how the asymmetry in the fact/value (and

Levels of Rationality		
Level I	Technical rationality	
Level II	Contextually-situated instrumental rationality	Instrumental reason
Level III	Practical rationality	Critical reason — practical = criticism
Level IV	Explanatory critical rationality	explanatory = critique
Level V	Depth-Explanatory-Critical rationality	Emancipatory reason
Level VI	Depth-rationality	
Level VII	Historical rationality	Historical reason

theory/practice) helices turn them into rational spirals. Figure 5 sketches the micro-logic of the theory/practice link. Among the five bases of actions, it is particularly facilities and opportunities that necessitate a politics as a concomitant to any therapy and a part of any emancipation. A definition of freedom shortly follows. To be free is (1) to know one's real interest; (2) to possess both (a) the ability and resources, i.e. generically the power, and (b) the opportunity to act in or towards them; and (3) to be disposed to do so. The possibility of depth explanations arise at each of the four limits on actors' knowledge. Note that criticism violates Hume's Law, but does not take us beyond the liberal's dilemma 'who knows how to judge and condemn the present, but not how to comprehend it'.

I now want to recapitulate my argument in *Scientific Realism and Human Emancipation*, moving through seven levels of reason, or better rationality, as summarized immediately above. At level I we have technical rationality – the use of the social sciences as sheer technique, and no interesting normative conclusions are entailed. At level II we have contextually situated instrumental rationality. Social science is no longer neutral in the context of relations of domination. For the dominated have an *interest* in knowledge that their oppressors may, and perhaps must, lack. Moving on to critical reason at level III we have intra-discursive (non-explanatory) critical or practical rationality. To say that a belief is false is to imply a negative evaluation on actions sustained or informed by the belief in question. All the sciences are intrinsically critical and so evaluative. All the sciences make judgements of truth or falsity on beliefs about their object domain. But the human sciences, in virtue of the distinctive feature of their domain, that it includes *inter alia* beliefs about social objects, also make (or at least entail) judgements of truth or falsity on aspects of that domain, in pursuing their explanatory charter.

I now want briefly to consider four objections to my core argument. (1) Even if 'P is false' is a value judgement, we are able to infer from it, together with explanatory premises, conclusions not intrinsic to every factual discourse. That truth is a good cannot be seized on as a concealed value premise to rescue the autonomy of value from factual discourse, without destroying the distinction between the two, the distinction that it is a point of the objection to uphold. (2) Even if all science presupposes values and if science is properly to be understood as a moral community, we are still able to infer from the premises of the explanatory-critical argument, conclusions which are not already implicit as anticipations in the organisation of scientific activity in general. (3) The fourth step in the inference scheme is not faulty. But diagnosis is not therapy and emancipated action will have a diferent logical form from emancipatory action. (4) Two gaps remain between step (iv) and action. First, that bridged by the *ceteris paribus* clause. The openness, diversity and historicity of social life necessitate this. These mediate the transition from the practical to what I have called the concrete axiological judgement. Second, the gap between this and a transformation in the agent's practice is bridged in the practical resolution of the theoretical problem of akrasia. Analytically, a transformation in the agent's praxis is followed by emancipatory action; transformative praxis – emancipating transformed transformative praxis involving the unity of auto- and alloplastic moments; then finally, emancipated free action. But it is important to note that this will still be determined – but now by wanted, needed and empowering structures rather than oppressive, unneeded and unwanted ones. Inference Scheme 1 can be generalized to show the genesis of cognitive illusions other than error; and to take in non-cognitive – practical and communicative – ills, including the non-satisfaction of practical and communicative goods, where as in Inference Scheme 4, these are conditions of discourse in general.[5]

I turn now to emancipatory reason. At level V – of depth explanatory critical rationality – simple models of depth-psychological rationalization and ideological mystification may be sketched. In the full development of the concept of ideology, facts about values, mediated by theories about facts, are transformed into values about facts, in the recognition *inter alia* that values themselves can be false. And we have a kind of axiological dialectic with Humean, explanatory critical and Spinozan moments.[6] At the first, Humean, moment some normative consensus, or widely shared set of values, is described; at the second, critical realist, moment the genesis or maintenance of the consensus is explained; and at the third, Spinozan, moment cognitively inappropriate values are transformed or eliminated in the praxis of the agents concerned. This may be dubbed the DET model, involving description, explanation and transformation. The second moment is not as novel as it may at first sight seem – in two respects. First, it has long – at least since Nietzsche – been realized that some values cannot be held consistently with a true account of their origin. Moreover, it has been appreciated tacitly that the critique of a scientific or proto-scientific theory in social science not only carries the trivial implication that one should not go on believing it, but involves an explanation of the reasons why it is believed and a critique of the circumstances which explain this. Marx's critique of political economy is a classic example of this kind. It has the structure of a triple critique. It is a critique of classical, political and vulgar economic theories; of lay beliefs, involving both practical and discursive consciousness, and of the categories and their schema which inform them; and of the structures, chiefly of the capitalist mode of production, underpinning them.

In ideology critique of the sort Marx's *Capital* exemplifies, three sorts of conditions – critical, explanatory and critical – must be satisfied. I elaborated them in *The Possibility of*

Naturalism, chapter 2 and *Scientific Realism and Human Emancipation*, chapter 3 and do not propose to comment further on them here. Instead, I move on to level VI – the depth rationality of the depth investigation. Here, the internal relation between explanatory theory and political or therapeutic emancipatory praxis comes into its own. Diagnosis, explanation and action follow each other in rapid concatenation. This is the DEA model of emancipation. In a sense it is just the transformational model of social activity applied to social values themselves. In it critical explanations will normally follow first the DREI scheme of theoretical and then the RRRE scheme of applied science,[7] which I have elaborated elsewhere. But it is important to stress that emancipation still involves choices and costs – thus dissonance, not liberation, may be the immediate effect of the DI (depth investigation). But the object of the DI is emancipation and the key question becomes: what are the conditions for the actualization of the powers of emancipated women and men? Five general conditions of the possibility of emancipatory practice may be indicated. First, reasons must be causes, or practical discourse is practically otiose. Secondly, values must already be present as latent tendencies, or normative discourse must be utopian or idle. Thirdly, critique must be internal to its objects, so social theory must be engaged and reflexive. Fourthly, there must be a coincidence of objective needs and subjective possibilities. And fifthly, emergent laws must operate for qualitative change to be possible. 'Emancipation depends upon explanation, depends upon emergence.' This appendix has attempted to situate only the abstract possibility of emancipation. Its practicality can only be ascertained by the concrete human sciences in depth investigations, doing moral philosophy as science.

NOTES

1 2nd edition, Hassocks, 1978.
2 This is also stressed by Anthony Giddens, in *Central Problems of Social Theory*, London, 1979, and elsewhere.

3 1st edition, Brighton, 1979.
4 See PON 1, pp. 73–4; PON 2, pp. 57–8.
5 See RR, chapter 6 for a full discussion of the Inference Schemes shown on p. 152 above.
6 Cf. A. Collier, *Socialist Reasoning*, London, 1990, chapter 4.
7 See SR, pp. 107–8.

Appendix 2

Marxist Philosophy from Marx to Althusser

In this appendix, I want to say something about Althusser's achievement as a Marxist philosopher by situating his work in the context of the itinerary of Marxist philosophy prior to it.[1]

It is now almost a commonplace to say that the tensions in Marxist thought – for example, between positivism and Hegelianism, social science and philosophy of history, scientific and critical Marxism, materialism and the dialectic – are rooted in the ambivalences and contradictory tendencies of Marx's own writings. Despite this, I think that it is possible to reconstruct from Marx's work positions in and on the theory of knowledge which transcend and partially explain the dichotomies within Marxist philosophy.

Two epistemological themes predominate in Marx:

α   An emphasis on *objectivity*, the independent reality of natural, and the relatively independent reality of social, forms with respect to their cognition (i.e. realism, in the ontological or 'intransitive' dimension).
β   An emphasis on the role of work or *labour* in the cognitive process, and hence on the social, irreducibly historical, character of its product, viz. knowledges (i.e. 'practicism', in the narrowly epistemological or 'transitive' dimension).

(α) is consistent with the practical modification of nature and constitution of social life; and Marx understands (β) as dependent on the mediation of intentional human agency or praxis. Objectification in both the senses of the production of a subject and of the reproduction or transformation of a social process must be distinguished both from objectivity *qua* externality, as in (α), and from the historically-specific, e.g. alienated, forms of labour in a particular society. It follows from this that 'objective' and its cognates have a fourfold meaning in Marx.[2] As developed by Marx, these two interrelated themes – of objectivity and labour – entail the epistemological supersession of empiricism and idealism, scepticism and dogmatism, hypernaturalism and anti-naturalism alike.

In his early writings Marx engaged a forceful and sporadically brilliant critique of idealism. This critique was the medium of his biographical *Ausgang* from philosophy into substantive socio-historical science,[3] and it provides us with the keys to the subject-matter of his new science. But he never undertook a comparable critique of empiricism. His anti-empiricism is available only in the methodological commitment to scientific realism implicit in *Capital*, together with a few scattered philosophical *aperçus*. Consequences of this critical imbalance have been the relative intellectual underdevelopment of the realist in comparison with the practicist pole within Marxist epistemology, amounting even to the denial (as we shall see shortly) that Marx is committed to the former, and a tendency for it to fluctuate between a sophisticated idealism (roughly practicism without realism) and a crude materialism (roughly realism without practicism).

Marx's critique of idealism, which incorporates a vigorous critique of rationalistic apriorism, consists in a double movement. In the first, Feuerbachian moment, ideas are treated as the products of finite embodied minds. This moment includes critiques of Hegel's subject–predicate inversions, the reduction of being to knowing (the 'epistemic fallacy') and the separation of philosophy from social life (the 'speculative illusion'). In the second, distinctively Marxian moment, these embodied minds are in turn conceived as at least partially the products of historically developing ensembles of social relations. In this anti-individualist moment, the Feuerbachian humanist or essentialist problematic of a fixed human nature is replaced by a problematic of an historically developing sociality, and/or of a human nature expressed only in it.[4] 'The human essence is no abstraction inherent in each single individual. In its reality it is the ensemble of social relations'.[5] 'The sum of the forces of production, capital and forms of social intercourse, which each individual confronts as something given, is the real foundation of . . . the "essence of man".'[6] At the same time, Marx wishes to insist that 'history is *nothing* but the activity of men in pursuit of their ends'.[7] Thus Marx works his way towards a conception of the reproduction and transformation of the social process in and through human praxis; and of praxis as in turn conditioned and made possible by that process. 'Men make their own history but they do not make it just as they please; they do not make it under circumstances chosen by themselves, but under circumstances directly encountered, given and transmitted by the past.'[8] Did Marx suppose that under communism men and women would make history as they pleased, that process would be dissolved into praxis? The evidence is ambiguous.[9] In any event, the subject-matter of *Capital* is not human praxis, but the structures, relations, contradictions and tendencies of the capitalist mode of production. 'Individuals are dealt with here only insofar as they are the personifications of economic categories, the bearers (*Träger*) of particular class relations and interests.'[10]

While Marx constantly affirms (1) *simple* (material object) *realism*, the idea that material objects exist independently of their knowledge, his commitment to (2) *scientific realism*, viz. the idea that the objects of scientific thought are real structures, mechanisms or relations ontologically irreducible to, normally out of phase with and perhaps in opposition to the phenomenal forms, appearances or events they generate, is arrived at only gradually, unevenly and relatively late – in fact *pari passu* with his deepening investigation of the capitalist mode of production. In the 1844 *Economic and Philosophical Manuscripts*, Marx, under the influence of Feuerbachian sensationalism, is critical of abstraction *per se*, and en route to the scientific realism of *Capital* toys with quasi-Kantian and quasi-

Leibnizian as well as with Hegelian and positivist views of abstraction. However, by the mid-1860s scientific realist motifs provide a constant refrain. 'All science would be superfluous if the outward appearances and essences of things directly coincided.'[11] 'Scientific truth is always paradox, if judged by everyday experience, which captures only the delusive appearance of things.'[12]

Despite the abundant textual evidence for Marx's continuing simple and his mature scientific realism, both are controversial. The latter has only relatively recently been recognized,[13] and an entire tradition has interpreted Marx as rejecting the former. This begins with Lukács's anathematization of any distinction between thought and being as a 'false and rigid duality',[14] Korsch's characterization of it as 'vulgar socialist' and Gramsci's dismissal of realism as a 'religious residue', and proceeds down to the extraordinary claims made on behalf of Marx by, e.g., Kolakowski that the very existence of things 'comes into being simultaneously with their appearance as a picture in the human mind'[15] and Schmidt that 'material reality is from the beginning socially mediated'[16] and that 'natural history is human history's extension backwards'.[17]

One reason for this is no doubt that Marx never brought into systematic relationship the two dimensions in terms of which he thought human knowledge, viz. the intransitive dimension of objectivity and the transitive dimension of practice. More especially, he never clearly set out the theoretical distinction (towards which he is groping in the 1857 *Grundrisse* Introduction) between two kinds of objects of knowledge, the transitive object of knowledge-production, which is a social product and actively transformed in the cognitive process, and the intransitive object of the knowledge produced, which is a (relatively or absolutely) independent, transfactually efficacious structure or mechanism.[18] Because Marx's originality lay in his concepts of praxis and of the labour process, it thus became easy for his realism to get lost or vulgarized or assimilated to that of some pre-existing philosophical tradition (e.g. Kantianism).

In opposition to vulgar economy, Marx claims to give a scientific, and in opposition to classical political economy a categorially adequate (non-fetishized, historicized), account of the real underlying relations, causal structures and generative mechanisms of capitalist economic life. Marx's method in fact incorporates three aspects:

1   a generic scientific realism;
2   a domain-specific, qualified (and critical) naturalism; and
3   a subject-particular dialectical materialism.

At (1), Marx's concern is, like that of any scientist, with a consistent, coherent, plausible and empirically-grounded explanation of his phenomena. At (2), his naturalism is qualified by a series of differentiae of social, as distinct from natural, scientific enquiry. The most important of these are the praxis- and concept-dependence and the greater space–time specificity of social forms, the historical reflexivity necessitated by the consideration that the critique of political economy is part of the process it describes and the fact that neither experimentally established nor naturally occurring closed systems are available for the empirical control of theory (entailing reliance on explanatory, non-predictive criteria of confirmation and falsification). (In this respect the 'power of abstraction', which Marx invokes in the Preface to the 1st edition of *Capital*, vol. I, neither provides a surrogate for 'microscopes' and 'chemical reagents' nor does justice to Marx's actual empirical practice.) At (3), the particular character of Marx's explanations is such that they take the form of an *explanatory critique* of an object of enquiry which is revealed, on those explanations, to be *dialectically contradictory*. Marx's scientific critique is both of (1) conceptual and conceptualized entities (economic theories and categories; phenomenal forms) and of (2) the objects (systems of structured relations) which necessitate or otherwise explain them. At the first level, the entities are shown to be false *simpliciter* (e.g. the wage form), fetishized (e.g. the value form) or otherwise defective. At the second level, Marx's explanations logically entail *ceteris paribus* a negative evaluation of the objects generating such entities and a commitment to their practical transformation. The particular systemic dialectical contradictions, such as between use-value and value, which Marx identifies as structurally constitutive of capitalism and its mystified forms of appearance give rise, on Marx's theory, to various historical contradictions which, on that theory, both tendentially subvert its principle of organization and provide the means and motive for its supersession by a society in which 'socialized mankind, the associated producers, regulate their interchange with nature rationally, [bringing] it under their conscious control, instead of being ruled by it as by some blind power'.[19] What bears stressing is the *contingently* critical nature of Marx's explanations and the *particularity* of the dialectical contradictions he identifies – both of which may be regarded as *empirically-grounded*, in virtue of the *a posteriori* character of Marx's theory as a whole.

If for Marx idealism is the typical fault of philosophy ('for which conceptual thinking is the real human being, and for which the conceptual world as such is the only reality'),[20] empiricism is the endemic failing of common sense, as exemplified, e.g., by 'the philistines' and vulgar economists' *way of looking at things* ... [which reflects] only the direct *form of manifestation* of relations ... not their *inner connection*'.[21] Marx sets himself against both conceptual and empirical realism: against both the idealist ontology of forms, ideas or notions with its conceptual (or religious) totalities and the empiricist ontology of given atomistic facts and their constant conjunctions; i.e. against both the 'ideal (heavenly) world' and the 'empirical (sensate) world' – in favour of the real world, conceived as structured, differentiated and developing and, given that we exist, a possible object of knowledge for us. Thus the essence of Marx's critique, in the *Theses on Feuerbach* (1845), of the old 'contemplative materialism' – whose objects are atomistic facts, contingently and constantly conjoined, apprehended by autonomized minds, the Robinsonades of epistemology – is that it desocializes and dehistoricizes science and destratifies reality; so that, at the very best, it can merely prompt, but not sustain '*scientificity*'. And the essence of

Marx's critique, in the final manuscript of the 1844 *Economic and Philosophical Manuscripts* and elsewhere, of the culmination of classical German idealism in the philosophy of Hegel is that it destratifies science and then dehistoricizes reality; so that it prompts, but cannot sustain, *'historicity'*. So we arrive at the twin epistemic motifs of Marx's new science of history: materialism signifying its generic form (as a science), dialectic its particular content (as a science of history). But it is an index of the epistemological lag of philosophical Marxism behind Marx that, whether fused in 'diamat' or separated in western Marxism, its dialectic has remained cast in an essentially idealist mould and its materialism expressed in a fundamentally empiricist form.

Marx (and Engels) usually associate dogmatism with idealism and rationalism, and scepticism with empiricism; and in *The German Ideology* (1845–6) they firmly reject both. Their premises, they announce, are not 'arbitrary dogmas' but can be verified 'in a purely empirical way'.[22] At the same time, they lampoon the kind of 'new revolutionary philosopher' who has 'the idea that men were drowned in water only because they were possessed with the *idea* of gravity'.[23] Thus, on the one hand (in the transitive dimension), they initiate the idea of Marxism as an empirically open-ended research programme; and, on the other (in the intransitive dimension), they register their commitment to an objective ontology of transfactually active structures.

Marx's position *on* epistemology also revolves around two interrelated themes: an emphasis (α) on the *scientificity* and (β) on the *historicity* of the cognitive process (the themes, of course, of the new science of history brought to bear on the theory of knowledge itself). On the one hand, Marx represents himself as engaged in the construction of a science, so that he is seemingly committed to certain epistemological propositions (e.g. criteria demarcating science from ideology or, say, art); and, on the other, he conceives all sciences, including his own, as a product of (and a potential causal agent in) historical circumstances, and must, therefore, be committed to the possibility of historically explaining them.

(α) and (β) constitute two aspects (the 'intrinsic' and 'extrinsic' aspects) of the cognitive process: (α) without (β) leads to *scientism* (or what Althusser will call 'theoreticism'), the dislocation of science from the socio-historical realm and a consequent lack of historical reflexivity; (β) without (α) results in *historicism*, the reduction of science to an expression of the historical process and a consequent judgemental relativism. These two aspects are united in the project of an explanatory critique of historically specific epistemologies.

However, the peculiar character of Marx's route from philosophy into science was such that here again, as in the case of his scientific realism, the nature of his commitment to the intrinsic aspect remained untheorised. Indeed, following a youthful early phase in which Marx visualizes the realization of philosophy in and through the proletariat, Marx's expressly articulated views on philosophy abruptly halt at a second positivist phase in which philosophy seems to be more or less completely superseded by science. 'When reality is depicted, philosophy as an independent branch of knowledge loses its medium of existence. At the best, its place can only be taken by the summing up of the most general results, abstractions which arise from the observation of the historical development of men.'[24] This abstract-summative conception of philosophy was given the imprimatur of the later Engels and became the orthodoxy of the Second International. However, there is a patent contradiction between Engels' theory and practice. His practice is that of an engaged *underlabourer* for historical materialism – a Lockean function which Marx clearly approved. Moreover, it is difficult to see how Marxism could dispense with epistemological interventions, and hence epistemological positions, so long as social conditions give rise not just to the (philosophical) 'problem of knowledge', but to knowledge as a (practical, historical) problem. In any event, if there is a third position implicit in Marx's practice, it is one in which philosophy (and *a fortiori* epistemology) is conceived as dependent upon science and other social practices – i.e. heteronomously, as a moment of a practical-cognitive ensemble. As such, it would have nothing in common with either the old

Hegelian 'German professorial concept-linking method' or the Lukácsian–Gramscian view of Marxism as a philosophy, rather than a (naturalistic) science, characterized by a totalizing vantage point of its own.

The main characteristics of the later Engels' immensely influential philosophical interventions were:

1 A conjunction of a positivistic conception of philosophy and a pre-critical metaphysics of the sciences.
2 An uneasy synthesis of a non-reductionist (emergentist) cosmology and a monistic (processual) dialectics of being.
3 Espousal of such a universal dialectical ontology in harness with a reflectionist epistemology, in which thought is conceived as mirroring or copying reality.
4 A vigorous critique of subjectivism and an emphasis on natural necessity combined with a stress on the practical refutation of scepticism.

Anti-Dühring (1876–8) was the decisive influence in the Marxism of the Second International, while the combination of a dialectics of nature and reflection theory became the hallmark of orthodox philosophical Marxism – styled 'dialectical materialism' by Plekhanov (following Dietzgen). Unfortunately, Engels' critique of the *contingency* of the causal connection was not complemented by a critique of its *actuality* (a notion shared by Hume with Hegel) or with co-equal attention to the mediation of natural necessities in social life by human praxes. Moreover, despite the great penetration Engels showed in his discussion of particular episodes in the history of science – e.g. his remarkable (post-Kuhnian!) Preface to *Capital*, vol. II (1884) – the effect of his reflectionism was the truncation of the transitive dimension and a regression to contemplative materialism. Thus the mainstream of the Second International, at its best in the works of Kautsky, Mehring, Plekhanov and Labriola, came to embrace a positivistic and rather deterministic evolutionism (in Kautsky's case, arguably more Darwinian than Marxian); and concerned itself for the most part with systematizing, rather than developing, the work of Marx and extending it to domains he had left untouched. Paradoxically, then, because if the main theme of Engels' intervention was materialism, his express intention had been to register and defend the specific autonomy of Marxism as a science, its outcome was a *Weltanschauung* not so very different from the hypernaturalist monisms – the 'mechanical' and 'reductive' materialisms – of Haeckel, Dühring et al., which Engels had set out to attack.

Lenin's distinctive contributions within the Engelsian framework were insistence on the practical and interested character of philosophical interventions and a clearer conception of the relative autonomy of such interventions from day-to-day science, both of which partially ameliorated the objectivist and positivist cast of Engels' thought. Lenin's philosophical thought moved through two phases: *Materialism and Empirio-Criticism* (1909) was a reflectionist polemic designed to counter the spread of Machian ideas in Bolshevik circles (e.g. by Bogdanov); while in *The Philosophical Notebooks* (1914–15), posthumously published in 1929, the Engelsian polar contrast between materialism and idealism gradually took second place to that between dialectical and non-dialectical thinking. There was a robust, if short-lived, debate in the Soviet Union in the 1920s between those, like Deborin, who emphasized the dialectical side and those, like Bukharin, who emphasized the materialist components of dialectical materialism. Thus the two terms of Engels' epistemological legacy – 'dialectics' and 'materialism' – were both rejected by Bernstein, were accentuated at different times by Lenin, externalized as an internal opposition within Soviet philosophy between Deborin and the mechanists, before its codification under Stalin as 'diamat'; henceforth they were to be represented by antithetical currents within Western Marxism.

In the thought of Max Adler and the Austro-Marxists, Marxian epistemology became self-consciously critical, in Kantian terms, in two senses: analogously, in that Marx, like Newton, had enabled the formulation of a Kantian question, viz. how is socialization possible? And directly, in that sociality was a condition of the possibility of experience in exactly the way that space, time and the categories are in Kant. For Adler, Marx's theory is to be understood as an empirically controlled critique, whose object – socialized humanity – is subject to quasi-natural laws, which depend for their operation upon intentional and value-oriented human activity.

None of the figures considered up to now doubted that Marxism was primarily a science (cf., e.g., Bukharin's *Historical Materialism* (1921)). At the same time, there was little, if any, emphasis on the authentically dialectical or Hegelian elements within Marx; for which, no doubt, the difficulty of Marx's exposition of the theory of value in *Capital* and the late publication of key early works were largely responsible. This situation now changed. Indeed, in the Hegelian Marxism expounded by Lukács in *History and Class Consciousness* (1923), which stimulated the work of the Frankfurt School and the genetic structuralism of Goldmann and provided an interpretative canon for Marx almost as influential as that of Engels, Korsch in *Marxism and Philosophy* (1923) and Gramsci in *The Prison Notebooks* (1929–35), the main emphases of the Engelsian tradition are diametrically and dramatically reversed.

The chief generic features of their theory of knowledge are (1) historicism, the identification of Marxism as the theoretical expression of the working class and of natural science as a bourgeois ideology, entailing the collapse of the intrinsic aspect of the cognitive labour process, together with rejection of Marxism as a social science in favour of Marxism as a self-sufficient or autonomous philosophy or social theory, with a comprehensive totalizing standpoint of its own; (2) anti-objectivism and anti-reflectionism, based on the idea of the practical constitution of the world, leading to the collapse or effective neutralization of the intransitive dimension of science and a corresponding epistemological idealism and judgemental relativism; (3) recovery of the subjective and critical aspects of Marxism (including in Lukács's case, the rediscovery of an essential ingredient of Marx's theory: the doctrine of fetishism), submerged in the positivistic scientism of the Second International.

Marxism is now fundamentally the expression of a subject, rather than the knowledge of an object – it is 'the theoretical expression of the revolutionary movement of the proletariat'.[25] Moreover, it is not just self-sufficient – containing as Gramsci puts it, 'all the fundamental elements needed to constitute a total and integral conception of the world'[26] – but distinguished precisely and only by this self-sufficiency. Thus for Lukács, 'it is not the primacy of economic motives that constitutes the decisive difference between Marxism and bourgeois thought, but the point of view of the totality [a position reiterated in his later *Ontology of Social Being*] ... the all-pervasive supremacy of the whole over its parts is the essence of the method which Marx took over from Hegel'.[27] From this standpoint natural science itself expresses the fragmentary, reified vision of the bourgeoisie, creating a world of pure facts, segregated into various partial spheres and unrelated to any meaningful totality. Thus Lukács inaugurates a long tradition within Marxism which (a) confounds science with its positivistic misrepresentation, and (b) starkly counterposes dialectical to analytical thought.

For Lukács the proletariat is the identical subject–object of history, and history (in the Lukácsian circle) is its realization of this fact. Historical materialism is nothing other than the self-knowledge of capitalist society, i.e. (on the circle) the ascribed consciousness of the proletariat – which, in becoming self-conscious, i.e. aware of its situation as the commodity on which capitalist society depends, already begins to transform it. Part 4 of Chapter 1 in *Capital*, vol. I on commodity fetishism 'contains within itself the whole of historical materialism, and the whole self-knowledge of the proletariat, seen as the knowledge of capitalist society'.[28] Lukács's epistemology is rationalist and his ontology idealist. More particularly, his totality is (as Althusser has pointed out) 'expressive', in that each moment or part implicitly contains the whole; and teleological, in that the present is only intelligible in relation to the future – of achieved identity – it anticipates. What the Marxian ontology has, and both the Engelsian ontology (highlighting process) and the Lukácsian ontology (highlighting totality) lack, is: *structure*. (This, as with complexity, differentiation and incompleteness is treated in the Second Book of Hegel's *Science of Logic* (1812–16) – on Essence – only to be spirited away into the self-explanatory philosophical realm of the Notion. But it is the unsublimated categories of Essence which, if one wants a Hegelian antecedent, dominate the discourse of *Capital*.)

For Gramsci the very idea of a reality-in-itself is a religious residue, and the objectivity of things is redefined in terms of a universal intersubjectivity of persons – i.e. as a cognitive consensus, asymptotically approached in history but only finally realized under communism, after a practical one has been achieved. Gramsci remarks that 'according to the theory of praxis it is clear that human history is not explained by the atomistic theory, but the reverse is the case: the atomistic theory, like all other scientific hypotheses and opinions, is part of the superstructure'.[29] This encapsulates a double collapse: of the intransitive to the transitive dimensions, and the intrinsic to the extrinsic aspects of science. In the first respect Gramsci's remark reminds one of Marx's jibe against Proudhon that, like 'the true idealist' he is, he no doubt believes that 'the circulation of the blood must be a consequence of Harvey's theory'.[30] The historicity of our knowledge (as well as the distinct historicity of its objects) on which Gramsci quite properly wishes to insist does not refute, but actually depends upon, the idea of the otherness of its objects (and their historicity).

Lukács, Gramsci and Korsch all reject any dialectics of nature of an Engelsian type, but whereas Lukács does so in favour of a dualistic, romantic anti-naturalism, Gramsci and Korsch do so in favour of a historicized anthropomorphic monism. Whereas Lukács argues that the dialectic, conceived as the process of the reunification of original subject and estranged object, only applies to the social world, Gramsci and Korsch maintain that nature, as we know it, is part of human history and therefore dialectical. While in Gramsci's achieved (being–knowing) identity theory, intransitivity is altogether lost, on Lukács's theory, on which identity is the still-to-be-achieved outcome of history, intransitivity remains in two guises:

1 as an epistemically inert nature, not conceived in any integral relation to the dialectic of human emancipation;
2 as the realm of alienation in human history, prior to the achievement of proletarian self-consciousness.

The principal epistemological themes of the 'critical theory' of Horkheimer, Adorno, Marcuse and (in a second generation) Habermas and their associates are (1) a modification of the absolute historicism of Lukácsian Marxism and a renewed emphasis on the relative autonomy of theory; (2) a critique of the concept of labour in Marx and Marxism; and (3) an accentuation of the critique of objectivism and scientism.

1 (1) is accompanied by a gradual decentring of the role of the proletariat and eventually results in the loss of any historically grounded agency of emancipation, so that – in a manner reminiscent of the young Hegelians against whom Marx and Engels polemicized – revolutionary theory is seen as an attribute of individuals (rather than as the expression of a class) and displaced onto the normative plane as a Fichtean '*Sollen*' or 'ought'. The consequent split between theory and practice, poignantly expressed by Marcuse – 'the critical theory of society possesses no concepts which could bridge the gap between present and future, holding no promise and showing no success, it remains negative'[31] – underscored a pessimism and judgementalism which, together with its totally negative – romantic and undialectical – conceptions of capitalism, science, technology and analytical thought, place its social theory – conceived as (as in historicist Marxism) the true repository of epistemology – at some remove from Marx's. By the same token, this allowed it to illuminate problems which Marx's own optimistic rationalism and Prometheanism had obscured.

2 The pivotal contrast of critical theory between an emancipatory and a purely technical or instrumental reason came

increasingly, from Horkheimer's 'Traditional and critical theory' (1937) to Habermas's *Knowledge and Human Interests* (1968), to be turned against Marx himself, in virtue of his emphasis on labour and his concept of nature purely as an object of human exploitation. Thus in *Eros and Civilisation* (1955) Marcuse conceives an emancipated society as one characterized neither by the rational regulation of necessary labour nor by creative work but rather by the sublimation of work itself in sensuous, libidinous play. According to Habermas, Marx recognizes a distinction between labour and interaction in his distinction between the forces and relations of production but misinterprets his own practice in a positivistic way, thereby reducing the self-formation of the human species to work. However, it may be argued that Marx understands labour not just as technical action, but as always occurring within and through an historically-specific society and that it is Habermas, not Marx, who mistakenly and uncritically adopts a positivistic account of labour, viz. as technical action, and more generally of natural science, viz. as adequately represented by the deductive-nomological model.

3 Habermas's attempt to combine a conception of the human species as a result of a purely natural process with a conception of reality, including nature, as constituted in and by human activity illustrates the antinomy of any transcendental pragmatism. For it leads to the dilemma that if nature has the transcendental status of a constituted objectivity it cannot be the historical ground of the constituting subject; and, conversely, if nature is the historical ground of subjectivity then it cannot simply be a constituted objectivity – it must be, to be blunt, *in-itself* (and, contingently, a possible object for us).[32] This is a point which Adorno, in his insistence on the irreducibility of objectivity to subjectivity, seems to have appreciated well. Indeed, in his *Negative Dialectics* (1966), Adorno isolates the endemic failing of First Philosophy, including Marxian epistemology, as the constant tendency to reduce one of a pair of mutually irreducible opposites to the other (e.g. in Engelsian Marxism consciousness to being, in Lukácsian Marxism being to consciousness) and

argues against any attempt to base thought on a non-presuppositionness foundation and for the immanence of all critique.

It will be convenient to treat together the work of (1) humanistic Marxists, such as E. Fromm, H. Lefebvre, R. Garaudy, A. Heller and E. P. Thompson; (2) existentialist and phenomenological Marxists, such as Sartre and Merleau-Ponty; (3) East European revisionists, such as L. Kolakowski, A. Schaff and K. Kosik; and (4) the Yugoslav praxis group of G. Petrović, M. Marković, S. Stojanović and their colleagues. Despite their diverse formations and preoccupations, all share a renewed emphasis on man and on human praxis as, in Petrović's words, 'the centre of authentic Marxist thought'[33] – an emphasis lost in the Stalinist era, whose recovery evidently owed much to the *Economic and Philosophical Manuscripts* (and, to a lesser extent, the new humanistic readings of Hegel's *Phenomenology* proposed by, e.g., A. Kojève and J. Hyppolite). Two points are worth stressing: first, it is assumed that human nature and needs, although historically mediated, are not infinitely malleable; secondly, the focus is on human beings not just as empirically given but as a normative ideal – as de-alienated, totalizing, self-developing, freely creative and harmoniously engaged. It is arguable that in the first respect at least this signals a partial return from Marx to Feuerbach. Among these writers, Sartre's *oeuvre* is the most far-reaching and sustained attempt to ground the intelligibility of history in that of individual human praxes. But, as has been noted before, Sartre's starting point logically precludes his goal. If real transformation is to be possible then a particular context, some specific ensemble of social relations, must be built into the structure of the individual's situation from the beginning. Otherwise one has: inexplicable uniqueness, a circular dialectic and the abstract a-historical generality of conditions (from 'scarcity' to the 'practico-inert').

By and large, anti-naturalist Western Marxism from Lukács to Sartre has shown little concern with either empirical confirmation or ontological structure. These biases are separately corrected in the scientific empiricism of Della Volpe and his school and the scientific rationalism of Althusser and other structuralist Marxists (such as M. Godelier).

If Lukács expresses the Hegelian current within Marxism in its purest form, Della Volpe draws out the positivist themes most exactly. The aim of his most important work, *Logic as a Positive Science* (1950), is the recovery of historical materialism as a tool of concrete empirically-oriented research and the revindication of Marxism as a materialist sociology or a 'moral Galileanism'. Della Volpe situates Marx's critique of Hegel as the historical climax of a line of materialist critiques of *a priori* reason extending from Plato's critique of Parmenides to Kant's critique of Leibniz. In it, Marx replaces the Abstract–Concrete–Abstract (A–C–A) Circle of the Hegelian dialectic with its 'indeterminate abstractions' by the Concrete–Abstract– Concrete (C–A–C or better C–A–C') Circle of materialist epistemology with its 'determinate rational abstractions', thus effecting a transition from 'hypostasis to hypothesis, from *a priori* assertions to experimental forecasts'.[34] 'Any knowledge worthy of the name is science'[35] and science always conforms to this schema, which Marx is said to have elaborated in the Introduction to the *Grundrisse*, and which, as Della Volpe interprets it, boils down to the familiar hypothetico-deductive model of Mill, Jevons, Popper and Hempel.

Only four kinds of problems with the Della Volpean reconstruction can be indicated here.

1 It is supposed to apply indifferently to social science and philosophy as well as natural science. The upshot is a hypernaturalist account of social science and a positivist-proleptic conception of philosophy shackled onto a view of science which is monistic and continuist within and across disciplines. This buttresses a conception of Marx's own development as linear and continuous.

2 C–A–C is a purely formal procedure which works equally well for many theoretical ideologies.

3 Della Volpe never clearly differentiates theoretical prece-

dents from historical causes: a latent historicism underpins the overt positivism of his work.

4 Most importantly, there are crucial ambiguities in the definition of the C–A–C′ model. Does 'C' refer to a conceptualized problem or a concrete object, i.e. does the circle describe a passage from ignorance or from being to knowledge? If it is designed to do both, then the consequent empirical realism, in tying together transitive and intransitive dimensions, destratifies reality and dehistoricizes knowledge. Does 'A' refer to something real, as in transcendental realism and Marx, or merely ideal, as in transcendental idealism and pragmatism? Finally, does 'C″' refer to (i) presentation, (ii) test, or (iii) application? The distinction between (i) and (ii) is that between Marx's order of presentation and enquiry; (ii) and (iii) that between the logics of theoretical and applied activity; (i) and (iii) that between the hierarchy of presuppositions of capitalist production elaborated in *Capital* and the kind of analysis of determinate historical conjunctures (the 'synthesis of many determinations' of the 1857 *Grundrisse* Introduction) which Marx essayed in the *18th Brumaire* (1852) or *The Civil War in France* (1871).

The best-known member of the Della Volpean school, Colletti, rejected even Della Volpe's restricted, purely epistemological, dialectics contending that any dialectic excluded materialism and criticized Della Volpe's hypernaturalist reconstruction of Marx for omitting the critical themes of reification and alienation. Colletti has, however, had great difficulty in reconciling these themes with his own unstratified empirical realist ontology and neo-Kantian conception of thought as other than being; and seems eventually to have settled on a split between the positive and critical dimensions of Marxism, thereby abandoning the notion of a scientific critique, before turning his back on Marxism itself. Colletti's work has also been criticized, e.g. by S. Timpanaro, for neglecting the ontological aspects of materialism.

This, then, in summary form, is the context in which I want to reconsider Althusser's achievement as a Marxist philosopher. Marxism is, here again, as it is with Della Volpe, the site of a *science* or a group of sciences (as well as in Althusser of a yet-to-be-produced philosophy). But it is now marked by a break from its antecedents. And the sciences have to do, as in Marx, with *structures* rather than events and with those events which are their *transformations*. Althusser's work falls into three distinct phases.[36] In Althusser one finds, most sharply formulated in his early programmatic and systematic (as distinct from his middle self-critical and late revisionary) works, and especially in the essays collected in *For Marx* (1965) and *Reading Capital* (1965):

1 A novel anti-empiricist and anti-historicist conception of the social totality. This pivots around his concept of 'overdetermination'.
2 A species of scientific rationalism. This is influenced by Spinoza,[37] the conventionalist 'historical epistemology' of the philosopher of science G. Bachelard[38] and the metapsychology of J. Lacan;[39] and generally steeped in the structuralist (and then post-structuralist) ambiance of the time. In Althusserian rationalism the intransitive dimension is effectively neutralised, resulting in a proleptic and latent idealism.
3 Rudiments of a critique of traditional epistemology coupled with a collapse, in his early work, of the extrinsic aspect of science ('theoreticism'). This is followed in his middle period by an emphasis on the heteronomy and partisan character of philosophy. It is then replaced in his final phase by a sociologistic historicist slide, in which now the intrinsic aspect of science is lost and epistemological categories are used only ironically.

1 Althusser reasserts the ideas of *structure* and *complexity*, on the one hand, and of *irreducible* (non-individualist) *sociality*, on the other, in his view of the social totality as an overdeter-

mined, decentred complex, pre-given whole, structured in dominance. Against empiricism, it is (a) a whole and (b) structured, and its form of causality is not Newtonian (mechanistic). Against historicism and holism it is (a) complex and (b) overdetermined, not an 'expressive totality', susceptible to an 'essential section' or characterized by a homogeneous temporality, and its form of causality is not Leibnizian (expressive). Against idealism, the social totality is pre-given; and against humanism – or, more appropriately, methodological individualism and essentialistic collectivism – its elements are structures and relations, not individuals or their aggregates, who are merely their bearers or occupants (*'Träger'*). Against sociological eclecticism or 'specialism', Althusser emphasizes that the totality is structured in dominance (thus it is the economy that determines which relatively autonomous level of the social totality is dominant), but his own positive concept of structural causality (the *Darstellung*) is only weakly elaborated.

In this constellation of ideas, it is probably the concept of 'overdetermination' that has proved to be of most importance. It signifies the multiple determination of events, structures and totalities, and of the contradictions which constitute, reproduce and transform them. In methodological terms it implies the need, in investigating any level or nexus of social reality, to search for internal and interconnectedly generated as well as external and analytically separable causes.

2   Althusser insists upon a distinction between the real and thought (and particularly in his second phase, stresses the priority of the real). But the former functions merely as a quasi-Kantian limiting concept within his system (as a kind of absolute reference point for thought). It thus, under pressure and in the hands of his post-structuralist successors, easily degenerates into an idealism, shedding the intransitive dimension completely, as e.g. in 'discourse theory'. It is significant that just as Althusser sees Spinoza, not Hegel, as the true precursor of Marx, his paradigm of science is mathematics, an apparently *a priori* discipline where the

crucial distinctions between the sense and reference of concepts and between the theory-dependence and theory-determination of data can be obscured. In short, Althusser tends to buy theory at the expense of experience. Similarly the limits of any natural science (e.g. physics) -based social science or history, or the specificy of the social sciences (let alone Marxist ones), are never explored. Althusser does not consider the distinctive geology or geography, or investigate the particular flora and fauna of the 'continent' of history, discovered or opened up by Marx.

3   Althusser is opposed, at least in his early period, to any reduction of philosophy to science or vice versa. But he insists that criteria of scientificity are completely internal to the science concerned. This raises two problems. First, what distinguishes science? Neither the counter-intuitive nor the open nor the disinterested character of scientific results or practices uniquely differentiate them from those of theoretical ideologies. Nor are these features necessarily characteristic of science. Secondly, what role is left for philosophy? Construction of a demarcation criterion between science and ideology, or critique of the practice of an alleged science seem ruled out by the stipulation of the purely internal criteriology of a science. Why then should the theory of theoretical practice not be given by a region of historical materialism, the sociology – rather than philosophy – of science? Philosophy is given a clearer role on Althusser's 'second definition'. It now represents the class struggle (i.e. politics) in theory (i.e. science) and conversely scientificity in politics,[40] but Althusser leaves the status of materialist philosophy's theses and the manner of their proof or vindication unclear.

At any rate, on the first definition, epistemological autonomy for the sciences is accompanied by and underpins their historical autonomy, and the ('theoreticist') dislocation of science from the historical process presupposes and implies the inevitability of ideology (conceived as mystification or false consciousness) and its function (the constitution of subjectivity) within it – a view, rightly or wrongly, at variance with Marx's. Moreover, as this function is necessary precisely so

that individuals may continue to perform their role of un-
consciously reproducing or tendentially transforming the
structures whose functionaries they are, the 'domination',
alongside the 'mystification', of agents by structures will remain under communism. Although Althusserian sociology
can pose the question of post-capitalist forms of determination, it ·cannot, it seems, give a non-alienating answer
to it: i.e. envisage, in a scientifically grounded way, structures which are more freely chosen, less opaque, more
empowering – because these categories are ideological (non-
scientific) ones. In sum, Althusser has purchased structure
at the price of praxis and the possibility of any (non-
voluntaristic, non-individualistic) scientific discourse about
human emancipation.

The emphases on the structural determination of multiply
determined phenomena investigated by cognitive disciplines –
sciences – impervious and unamenable to political manipulation and control led to a great flowering of social-scientific and
historical research in the tradition inaugurated by Marx.[41]
Whatever its internal weaknesses and susceptibility to critical
realist critique, in recasting Marx's thinking about itself,
science and society, Louis Althusser made a contribution
of decisive importance. The Althusserian legacy demands
nothing less than the most thorough-going critical reappro-
priation today.

NOTES

1   In this appendix I have drawn heavily on my article 'Know-
    ledge, theory of' in *A Dictionary of Marxist Thought*, ed. T.
    Bottomore et al. Oxford, 1983, pp. 254–63 reproduced with
    modifications in *Reclaiming Reality*, chapter 7–3. My thanks are
    due to Basil Blackwell and to Tom Bottomore for permission to
    use material originally published therein. In reconstructing the
    pre-Althusserian history of Marx's philosophy I have freely but
    critically used Althusserian insights, exemplifying the process
    which Bachelard called 'recurrence', the rewriting of scientific,
    or more generally intellectual/cultural, history after a structural

break. (For an introductory account, see D. Lecourt, *Marxism and Epistemology*, London, 1975, pp. 84–6 and passim).

2 Cf. C. Arthur, *Dialectics of Labour*, Oxford, 1986, chapter 1 and passim.

3 Cf. G. Labica, *Marxism and the Status of Philosophy*, Brighton, 1980.

4 Cf. N. Geras, *Marx and Human Nature: Refutation of a legend*, London, 1983.

5 *Concerning Feuerbach*, Thesis VI, *Early Writings*, Harmondsworth, 1979, p. 423.

6 *The German Ideology*, vol. 1, part 1, section 7 – *Collected Works*, vol. 5, London, 1976, p. 54.

7 *The Holy Family*, chapter VI, part 2.

8 'The 18th Brumaire of Louis Bonaparte', *Selected Works*, London, 1968, p. 97.

9 See my 'Determinism', *A Dictionary of Marxist Thought*, pp. 117–19.

10 *Capital*, vol. 1, Preface to the first edition.

11 *Capital*, vol. 3, chapter 48.

12 *Value, Price and Profit*, part VI.

13 See my PON; D. Sayer, *Marx's Method*, Brighton, 1979; and *Issues in Marxist Philosophy*, vols I–III, eds J. Mepham and D.-H. Ruben, Brighton, 1979.

14 G. Lukács, *History and Class Consciousness*, London, 1971, p. 204.

15 L. Kolakowski, *Marxism and Beyond*, London, 1958, p. 69.

16 A. Schmidt, *The Concept of Nature in Marx*, London, 1971, p. 35.

17 Ibid.

18 See my RTS, especially chapters 1 and 2. For comment on the relationship between this realist distinction and the Althusserian one between the object of knowledge and the real object, see my RR, chapter 9, p. 188.

19 *Capital*, vol. III, chapter 48.

20 *Grundrisse*, Introduction, part 3.

21 *Letter to Engels*, 27 June 1867.

22 *The German Ideology*, vol. I, part 1,a.

23 Ibid., Preface.

24 *The German Ideology*, vol. I, part 1,a.

25 K. Korsch, *Marxism and Philosophy*, London, 1970, p. 42.

26 A. Gramsci, *The Prison Notebooks*, London, 1971, p. 462.

27 G. Lukács, *History and Class Consciousness*, London, 1971, p. 27.

28 Ibid., p. 170.

29 Gramsci, *Prison Notebooks*, p. 465.

30 K. Marx, *The Poverty of Philosophy*, chapter 2, section 3.

31 H. Marcuse, *One-dimensional Man*, London, 1968, p. 257.

32 Cf. T. McCarthy, *The Critical Theory of Jürgen Habermas*, London, 1978, p. 111.

33 *Praxis* vol. I (1967), p. 64.

34 G. Della Volpe, *Logic as a Positive Science*, London, 1980, p. 198.

35 G. Della Volpe, *Rousseau and Marx*, London, 1978, p. 200.

36 For a detailed and judicious account of his career, see G. Elliott, *Althusser: The Detour of Theory*, London, 1987; and for an illuminating comparison of his philosophy with that of transcendental realism, see A. Collier, *Scientific Realism and Socialist Thought*, Hemel Hempstead, 1989.

37 See L. Althusser, 'Elements of self-criticism', *Essays in Self-Criticism*, London, 1976, pp. 132ff. Cf. P. Anderson, *Considerations on Western Marxism*, London, 1976, pp. 64–6.

38 See T. Benton, *The Rise and Fall of Structural Marxism*, London, 1984, pp. 23 – 31 for an introduction and my 'Feyerabend and Bachelard', *New Left Review* 94 (1975), pp. 47–55 (reprinted in my RR, chapter 3, pp. 41–8) for a critique.

39 See A. Lemaire, *Jacques Lacan*, London, 1977, for an introductory exposition and P. Dews, *Logics of Disintegration*, London, 1987, especially chapters 2 and 3 for a sympathetic critique.

40 See 'Lenin and philosophy', *Lenin and Philosophy*, London, 1971, chapter 2.

41 See the careful documentation of the positive legacy of (especially high) Althusserianism in Elliott, *Althusser*, pp. 324ff.; and cf. P. Anderson, *Arguments within English Marxism*, London, 1980, p. 126.

General Index

Name Index

Index compiled by Meg Davies (Society of Indexers)